THE
EARTH SPEAKS

AN ACCLIMATIZATION JOURNAL

·J. MUIR·

P9-CJJ-033

EDITED BY
STEVE VAN MATRE
AND BILL WEILER

DESIGNED AND PRODUCED BY
SYCAMORE ASSOCIATES

Cover and Frontispiece by Jan Muir

Blockprints Copyright © by
Gwen Frostic, Presscraft Papers, Benzonia, Michigan 49616

Thirteen printings through July, 1997

Acknowledgments for selections are on pages 186-187.

Printed on recycled paper.

ISBN: 0-917011-00-7

Library of Congress: 83-070349

Published By

THE INSTITUTE FOR EARTH EDUCATION
CEDAR COVE
GREENVILLE, WV 24945
U.S.A.

DEDICATED

to the marsh
at Camp Towering Pines
where Acclimatization was born
many years ago.

TABLE OF CONTENTS.

EARTH MAGIC

EARTH WISDOM

EARTH SPIRIT

In Appreciation

What can you say in a few lines about Gwen Frostic?
That the earth spoke to her, that she listened and shared
what she heard, that she has lived her life capturing and
reproducing the beauty of our preeminent home. I have
no doubt that she's a household word where it really
counts, among the fellow passengers with whom we
share this planet. In a way, Gwen has become the
spokesperson for the real common folk of the earth: the
flowers and trees, the small birds and other animals, the
bugs, the ferns, the toadstools.

Gwen's work is a wonderful example of that love affair
with the natural world that we wish to nourish. Her
eloquent images have given all of us a chance to
endlessly enjoy the fleeting moments with which nature
builds an unfolding natural world. We were overjoyed
when she allowed us to use her wood engravings to
illustrate the thoughts reproduced on these pages.

Gwen's images and words have already touched the lives
of tens of thousands of people. For her old friends we
hope this book will be another treasure; for newcomers,
please write to Gwen for a catalog of her work. You will
be glad you did.

Let's just wander here and there _ _ _ _
like leaves floating in the autumn air
and look at common little things _ _ _ _ _
stones on the beach _ _ _
flowers turning into berries . . .
. . . from the winds we'll catch a bit
of that wondrous feeling that comes _ _ _
_ _ not from seeing _ _ _ _
but from being part of nature . . .

— Gwen Frostic

ACKNOWLEDGMENTS

THE EARTH SPEAKS represents the fulfillment of a dream of many years. Harry Hoogesteger set the stage when he compiled a collection of readings to use on a natural awareness camping experience that we called the Seton Journey in *Acclimatizing*.

Bill Weiler is another of those wonderful, selfless individuals who have consistently appeared to keep the larger dream of Acclimatization alive. He mobilized dozens of our members to assist in seeking out and sifting through the hundreds of possible quotes and passages we were to end up with. Bill wrote all the necessary letters pleading with the various authors and publishers and heirs to assist us in our undertaking. He then quietly shepherded the assembled pieces and participants and patiently waited out all my delays as the press of workshops and other tasks created seemingly endless postponements.

Jim Wells once again handled the mechanics, including the layout and design, and took charge of all those last-minute details that must be attended to and worried over. Finally, Bill Hart's timely support allowed us to obtain a crucial story, Loren Eiseley's "How Flowers Changed the World." All who read THE EARTH SPEAKS owe these folks a debt of gratitude.

PREFACE

It was one of the coldest winters in Chicago's history nearly eighteen seasons ago when the idea of this book was first mentioned to me. Since then, a mountain-full of correspondence has flowed in and out of my home in order that THE EARTH SPEAKS could become a reality.

This endeavor has truly been a group effort, a group journey.

Steve Van Matre has been the main mover of the book. My meetings with him always resulted in an energetic surge of output and a comforting realization that THE EARTH SPEAKS would indeed become a finished work.

To Gwen Frostic, I owe the deepest of thanks. The difficult task of finding an artist to match the matchless writings was accomplished when she volunteered her boundless talents for this project.

Jim Wells, Jan Muir, and Kirk Hoessle, staff of Sycamore Associates, a professional interpretive planning and design firm, volunteered much of their time in the design, layout and production of the book. They have done an excellent job in blending the writings and the artwork to bring the book to life. I'm very grateful for all that they have contributed.

The rest of the members and friends listed below have their own stories and their own magic to share which can be found throughout these pages. The noble spirit of each is best described by the last words of the *Jumping Mouse* story.

Cyndi Cashman	Jeff McFadden	Dave Siegenthaler
Sarah Davis	Karla McGee	Eddie Soloway
Michael Dempster	Corky McReynolds	Paul Stetzer
Donn Edwards	Nancy Messmer	Bill Staunton
Dave Falvo	Mike Mayer	Mark Thomas
Laurie Farber	Helene Phelps	Roger Tucker
Susan Gardner	Jeff Post	Renate Tucker
Marc Harvey	Bill Reynolds	Ginger Wallis
Mary Knight	Gloria Sarin	Dave Wampler
Karen Gartland	Scott Schrage	Rene Knight Weiler
		Julie Wieters

— Bill Weiler
Mt. Hood, Oregon

INTRODUCTION

This summer I traveled around the world talking about
our Acclimatization programs, and as I circled the earth,
I listened to both its natural and human voices. There is
no doubt, the earth is in trouble. In our quest to be gods
we have rent the very fabric of life. Everywhere the
voices of despair are clear. Yet the voices of hope are
there, too. Wherever I went I found people concerned
about the earth. It is upon this concern that we must
build for tomorrow.

For those unfamiliar with our work, Acclimatization is
the name of a special process a group of us developed
for helping people build a sense of relationship — in
both feelings and understandings — with the natural
world. It is a way of getting others to tune in and turn
on to our magical planet and its systems of life. For over
a decade now, Acclimatization activities and programs
have represented some of the most widely used materials
in the general field of nature education.

THE EARTH SPEAKS is our collection of images and
impressions recorded by those who lived in close contact
with the natural world; those who discovered its essence
and were able to capture on paper the magic and
meaning of that discovery. The journal contains the
writings of naturalists and natives, poets and
philosophers, scientists who went beyond analysis to
"seeing," and ordinary people who were able to discover
for themselves how life works on this planet and what
that might mean for themselves and their children.

The purpose of our Acclimatization journal is to spotlight the importance and joy of cultivating a sense of earth magic, to emphasize the urgent need to seek out and act upon words of earth wisdom, and to refresh and recharge an inner feeling of earth spirit. The journal is also a tool for reawakening that sense of wonder we all had as youngsters, that sense of awe in the presence of the mysteries of life. We think you will find many of your favorite quotes and passages here, along with lots of new ones, and perhaps even a few surprises.

We hope THE EARTH SPEAKS will be read by individuals in moments of solitude, shared among friends around trailside campfires, and used by leaders to intensify their feelings for the natural world as they prepare to help their learners develop a love for life and the systems of the earth that sustain it. If the journal is successful, it should prove to be both thought provoking and uplifting for the reader.

We have selected these passages, not because all these writers would have agreed with us, but because each in some way speaks for the earth. Whether read in the crisp light of early morning, or the glow of a single candle by a dying campfire, we believe the journal shines with the wisdom and love of individuals who have touched the natural world and have, in turn, been deeply touched by it.

Those of us involved in Acclimatization hope that THE EARTH SPEAKS will serve in a small way to help people renew their sense of relationship with the earth while we still have a chance to control our destiny. Come, listen to the earth with us.

S.V.M.
Great Barrier Reef
August, 1982

EARTH MAGIC

EARTH MAGIC

Steve Van Matre

HAVE YOU LISTENED TO THE EARTH?

Yes, the earth speaks, but only to those who can hear with their hearts. It speaks in a thousand, thousand small ways, but like our lovers and families and friends, it often sends its messages without words. For you see, the earth speaks in the language of love. Its voice is in the shape of a new leaf, the feel of a water-worn stone, the color of evening sky, the smell of summer rain, the sound of the night wind. The earth's whispers are everywhere, but only those who have slept with it can respond readily to its call.

The earth speaks in many ways, on many levels. For the Australian Aboriginals, perhaps the oldest continuous culture in the world, the features of the earth are an everyday part of their living heritage. They read their story of life in the landscape itself. For them every mountain, every river, every valley speaks of ancient events. A gigantic monolith becomes a rock dropped from the sky, a stone outcropping an effigy figure, a mountain range a great lizard. For the modern geologist, the earth speaks of ancient events as well, but in this instance, those features are the direct result of the natural phenomena of the planet. A hill represents a glacial remnant, a solitary boulder an erratic, a canyon a timetable. However, for the earth lover, each fold, each depression, each peak in the crust of the planet speaks of new discoveries in a lifelong quest to seek out magical places, to be intimate with the earth and its life.

Yes, falling in love with the earth is one of life's great adventures. It is an affair of the heart like no other; a rapturous experience that remains endlessly repeatable throughout life. This is no fleeting romance, it's an uncommon affair, one that is unconstrained by age or custom, and strengthened rather than diminished through sharing. In fact, the more one gives it away, the stronger it grows.

Come, listen to the earth. For our opening section we have collected the thoughts and insights of several people who have heard the earth's song. Some are exuberant like Burroughs and Muir, others more reflective like Thoreau and Olson, or instructive like Carson and Beston, but they are all great lovers, lovers of the earth and its life.

The earth speaks in magic, the magic of rainbows and waterfalls and frogs. It is the magic of interacting sunlight and air and water and soil creating a constantly shifting kaleidoscope of wondrous riches on our turning planet. In fact, for someone visiting earth for the first time, the real treasures here would all be free. The smell of a sunlit prairie, the taste of a cold cup of spring water, the crunch of trackless snow underfoot, these are some of the earth's supreme treasures. On intergalactic maps, if there are such things, the place where we live must surely be designated as a magical garden in space, a place of astounding beauty. Picture for a moment people arriving here in a rather sterile, lifeless spaceship. For them the earth would certainly be a precious oasis in the cosmos. Such space travelers would know the earth as a place to quench their thirst for the wonders of life itself, a stopping point for sustenance beyond the necessities of food and water. They would no doubt travel great distances to marvel at what we have here, to discover anew this amazing source of adventure and inspiration and joy. There must be many worlds where we would be envied greatly for our good fortune, worlds where the conditions for life are much harsher. Yet ironically, there are those among us who suggest that because we are fouling our home we should dream of getting off. If there are intergalactic travelers likely to visit us, will we not also be seen as childish fools who could not control our appetites?

Come experience the earth with us. Set aside some time each week to get to know your place in space. In addition to being a day of rest, perhaps Sunday should be a day of exploration and discovery for all of us. We need a day dedicated to getting out of our man-made structures, to leaving our urban colonies; a day spent outdoors celebrating the wonders of life; a day cavorting, if you will, in our garden in space.

There's a magical story about St. Francis enjoying the night air one evening in the village of Assisi. When the moon came up, it was huge and luminous, bathing the entire earth in radiance. Noticing that no one else was outside to enjoy this miracle, Francis ran to the bell tower and began ringing the bell enthusiastically. When the people rushed from their houses in alarm and saw Francis at the top of the tower, they called out asking him to explain what was wrong. Francis replied simply, *"Lift up your eyes, my friends. Look at the moon!"*

Sometimes all that is necessary for hearing the earth's voice is just to get out of our boxes like the people of Assisi did one memorable evening. But often, it means going farther away from the world of people, casting off layers of the synthetic and artificial substances with which we have encased ourselves. We have listened too long solely to the voices of our own kind when, in reality, we share this vessel with a grand multitude of other forms of life. Since they do not speak our language, we must seek them out and learn theirs:

> "But ask now the beasts,
>   and they shall teach thee;
> and the fowls of the air,
>   and they shall teach thee;
> Or speak to the earth,
>   and it shall teach thee;
> And the fishes of the sea
>   shall declare unto thee.
>   JOB 12:7-8

The point is, we desperately need to put aside our human acquaintances for a while (and yes, our books, too) and go away from the world of words, to communicate on a different level, to get close enough, as Abbey suggests (in a section from *The Journey Home* included here), to learn what the mountain lion has to teach us.

Although the earth speaks to everyone, only a few

respond. Sadly, there are many among us who can no longer hear the earth's song. They have lost their innate abilities to perceive its underlying harmony; they have become entrapped by their own contrivances. Consider the example of an obviously bored teenager rounding the corner of a zig-zagging trail along the Big Sur Coast of California and exclaiming in a whiny voice, "Awwoh, it's the same view." Faced with indescribable beauty this young traveler could only complain that she had seen it before. Standing on the threshold of what could well be the most lasting love affair of her life, she was unable to sense her lover's charms. We have so filled our lives with artificial nonsense and distraction that many of us can no longer hear the earth's voice. We need new teachers to help us rebuild a sense of relationship with the earth, and to remind us, as Li Po suggests in the final lines of this section, to loosen our hair and go fishing.

Come, listen to the earth with us. For those who have learned to hear its song the earth can soothe the troubled heart, refresh the weary, soften the hardened, redirect the lost. And in the end, it is unlikely that you will ever find an earth lover holed up in some sterile urban box slowly withering away — withdrawn, sad, bitter. Earth lovers retain their vigor, their zest for life. For them the natural world remains an inexhaustible source of delight: the sounds, textures, colors, shapes, patterns, harmonies; the sensate joy, the enchantment, the endless surprises. Earth lovers know that no man-made setting can ever hope to attain the richness, the drama, the meaning found in most any patch of wild land. Like a bottomless well in our oasis in space, the wonders of the earth can be drawn upon to recharge the spirit for all of one's days. Be an earth lover. Sleep with the earth. It will teach thee.

Ralph Waldo Emerson

The earth laughs
in flowers.

John
Burroughs

LEAF AND TENDRIL

I am bound to praise the simple life, because I have lived it and found it good. When I depart from it, evil results follow. I love a small house, plain clothes, simple living. Many persons know the luxury of a skin bath — a plunge in the pool or the wave unhampered by clothing. That is the simple life — direct and immediate contact with things, life with the false wrappings torn away — the fine house, the fine equipage, the expensive habits, all cut off. How free one feels, how good the elements taste, how close one gets to them, how they fit one's body and one's soul! To see the fire that warms you, or better yet, to cut the wood that feeds the fire that warms you; to see the spring where the water bubbles up that slakes your thirst, and to dip your pail into it; to see the beams that are the stay of your four walls, and the timbers that uphold the roof that shelters you; to be in direct and personal contact with the sources of your material life; to want no extras, no shields; to find the universal elements enough; to find the air and the water exhilarating; to be refreshed by a morning walk or an evening saunter; to find a quest of wild berries more satisfying than a gift of tropic fruit; to be thrilled by the stars at night; to be elated over a bird's nest, or over a wild flower in spring — these are some of the rewards of the simple life.

Walt Whitman

LEAVES OF GRASS

Now I see the secret of the making of the best persons. It is to grow in the open air, and to eat and sleep with the earth.

John Muir

*T*his *grand show* is eternal. It is always sunrise somewhere; the dew is never all dried at once; a shower is forever falling; vapor is ever rising. Eternal sunrise, eternal sunset, eternal dawn and gloaming, on sea and continents and islands, each in its turn, as the round earth rolls.

Byrd
Baylor

"THE WAY TO START A DAY"

The way to start a day is this —
Go outside and face the east and greet the sun
with some kind of blessing or chant or song
that you made yourself and keep for early morning.
The way to make the song is this —
Don't try to think what words to use
until you're standing there alone.
When you feel the sun
you'll feel the song, too.
Just sing it.

But don't think you're the only one who ever
    worked that magic.
Your caveman brothers knew what to do.
Your cavewoman sisters knew, too.
They sang to help the sun come up.
and lifted their hands to its power.
A morning needs to be sung to.

A new day needs to be honored.
People have always known that.
Didn't they chant at dawn in the sun temples of
    Peru?
And leap and sway to Aztec flutes in Mexico?
And drum sunrise songs in the Congo?
And ring a thousand small gold bells in China?
Didn't the pharaohs of Egypt say the only sound at
    dawn
should be the sound of songs that please the
    morning sun?
They knew what songs to sing.
People always seemed to know.

And everywhere they knew what gifts the sun
    wanted.
In some places they gave gold.
In some places they gave flowers.
In some places, sacred smoke blown to the four
    directions.
Some places, feathers and good thoughts.
Some places, fire.
But everywhere they knew to give *something*.

And everywhere they knew to turn their faces
    eastward
as the sun came up.
Some people still know.
When the first pale streak of light cuts through the
    darkness,
wherever they are,
those people make offerings

and send mysterious strong songs to the sun.
They know exactly how to start a day.

Their blessings float on the wind over Pueblo
    cornfields
in New Mexico, and you hear their morning songs
in villages in Africa,
and they salute the sunrise ceremonially
in the high cold mountains of Peru.
Today long before dawn
they were already waiting in Japan with prayers
and they were gathering at little shrines in India
with marigolds in their hands.

They were bathing in the sacred Ganges River as
    the sun came up.
And high on a mesa in Arizona
they were holding a baby toward the sun.
They were speaking the child's new name
so the sun would hear and know that child.
It had to be sunrise.
And it had to be that first sudden moment.
That's when all the power of life is in the sky.

Some people say there is a new sun every day,
that it begins its life at dawn
and lives for one day only.
They say you have to welcome it.
You have to make the sun happy.
You have to make a good day for it.
You have to make a good world for it
to live its one-day life in.

And the way to start, they say,
is just by looking east at dawn.
When they look east tomorrow,
you can too.
Your song will be an offering —
    and you'll be one more person
in one more place
at one more time in the world
saying hello to the sun,
letting it know you are there.

If the sky turns a color sky never was before
just watch it.
That's part of the magic.
That's the way to start a day.

Robert
Service

"THE CALL OF THE WILD"

Have you gazed on naked grandeur where
there's nothing else to gaze on,
Set pieces and drop-curtain scenes galore,
Big mountains heaved to heaven, which the
blinding sunsets blazon,
Black canyons where the rapids rip and roar?
Have you swept the visioned valley with
the green stream streaking through it,
Searched the Vastness for a something you
have lost?
Have you strung your soul to silence? Then
for God's sake go and do it;
Hear the challenge, learn the lesson, pay the cost.

Have you wandered in the wilderness, the sagebrush
desolation,
The bunch-grass levels where the cattle graze?
Have you whistled bits of rag-time at the end
of all creation,

And learned to know the desert's little ways?
Have you camped upon the foothills, have you
galloped o'er the ranges,
Have you roamed the arid sun-lands through and
    through?
Have you chummed up with the mesa? Do you
know its moods and changes?
Then listen to the Wild — it's calling you.

Have you known the Great White Silence, not
a snow-gemmed twig aquiver?
(Eternal truths that shame our soothing lies.)
Have you broken trail on snowshoes? mushed
your huskies up the river,
Dared the unknown, led the way, and
clutched the prize?
Have you marked the map's void spaces,
mingled with the mongrel races,
Felt the savage strength of brute in every thew?
And though grim as hell the worst is, can you
round it off with curses?
Then harken to the Wild — it's wanting
you.

Have you suffered, starved and triumphed,
groveled down, yet grasped at glory,
Grown bigger in the bigness of the whole?
"Done things" just for the doing, letting babblers
tell the story,
Seeing through the nice veneer the naked soul?
Have you seen God in His splendors, heard the
text that nature renders?
(you'll never hear it in the family pew.)

The simple things, the true things, the silent
men who do things —
Then listen to the Wild — it's calling you.

They have cradled you in custom, they have
primed you with their preaching,
They have soaked you in convention through
and through;
They have put you in a showcase; you're a
credit to their teaching —
But can't you hear the Wild? — it's calling
you.
Let us probe the silent places, let us seek what
luck betide us;
Let us journey to a lonely land I know.
There's a whisper on the night-wind, there's
a star agleam to guide us,
And the Wild is calling, calling . . . let us
go.

John
Muir

C limb the mountains and get their good tidings. Nature's peace will flow into you as sunshine flows into trees. The winds will blow their own freshness into you, and the storms their energy, while cares will drop off like autumn leaves.

Gary
Snyder

RIPRAP AND COLD MOUNTAIN POEMS

I settled at Cold Mountain long ago,
Already it seems like years and years.
Freely drifting, I prowl the woods and streams
And linger watching things themselves.
Men don't get this far into the mountains,
White clouds gather and billow.
Thin grass does for a mattress,
The blue sky makes a good quilt.
Happy with a stone underhead
Let heaven and earth go about their changes.

Hokushi

THE FOUR SEASONS: JAPANESE HAIKU

Experimenting . . .
I hung the moon
on various
branches of the pine

Henry Beston

"THE YEAR AT HIGH TIDE"

Had I room in this book, I should like to write a whole chapter on the sense of smell, for all my life long I have had of that sense an individual enjoyment. To my mind, we live too completely by the eye. I like a good smell — the smell of a freshly ploughed field on a warm morning after a night of April rain, the clovelike aroma of our wild Cape Cod pinks, the morning perfume of lilacs showery with dew, the good reek of hot salt grass and low tide blowing from these meadows late on summer afternoons.

What a stench modern civilization breathes, and how have we ever learned to endure that foul blue air? In the Seventeenth Century, the air about a city must have been much the same air as overhung a large village; today the town atmosphere is to be endured only by the new synthetic man.

Our whole English tradition neglects smell. In

English, the nose is still something of an indelicate organ, and I am not so sure that its use is not regarded as somewhat sensual. Our literary pictures, our poetic landscapes are things to hang on the mind's wall, things for the eye. French letters are more indulgent to the nose; one can scarcely read ten lines of any French verse without encountering the omnipresent, the inevitable *parfum*. And here the French are right, for though the eye is the human master sense and chief aesthetic gate, the creation of a mood or of a moment of earth poetry is a rite for which other senses may be properly invoked. Of all such appeals to sensory recollection, none are more powerful, none open a wider door in the brain than an appeal to the nose. It is a sense that every lover of the elemental world ought to use, and, using, enjoy. We ought to keep all senses vibrant and alive. Had we done so, we should never have built a civilization which outrages them, which so outrages them, indeed, that a vicious circle has been established and the dull sense grown duller.

One reason for my love of this great beach is that, living here, I dwell in a world that has a good natural smell, that is full of keen, vivid, and interesting savours and fragrances. I have them at their best, perhaps, when hot days are dulled with a warm rain. So well do I know them, indeed, that were I blindfolded and led about the summer beach, I think I could tell on what part of it I was at any moment standing. At the ocean's very edge the air is almost always cool — cold even — and delicately moist with surf spray and the endless dissolution of the innumerable bubbles of the foam slides; the wet sand slope beneath exhales a cool savour of mingling beach and sea, and the innermost breakers push ahead of them puffs of this fragrant air. It is a singular experience to walk this brim of ocean when the wind is blowing almost directly down the beach, but now veering a point toward the dunes, now a point toward the sea. For twenty feet a humid and tropical exhalation of hot, wet sand encircles one, and from this one steps, as through a door, into as many yards of mid-September. In a point of time, one goes from Central America to Maine.

Atop the broad eight-foot back of the summer bar, inland forty feet or so from the edge of low tide, other odours wait. Here have the tides strewn a moist table-land with lumpy tangles, wisps, and matted festoons of ocean vegetation — with common sea grass, with rockweed olive-green and rockweed olive-brown, with the crushed and wrinkled green leaves of sea lettuce, with edible, purple-red dulse and bleached sea moss, with slimy and gelatinous cords seven and eight feet long. In the hot noontide they lie, slowly, slowly withering — for their very substance is water — and sending an odour of ocean and vegetation into the burning air. I like this good natural savour. Some-times a dead, surf-trapped fish, perhaps a dead skate curling up in the heat, adds to this odour of vegetation a faint fishy rankness, but the smell is not earth corruption, and the scavengers of the beach soon enough remove the cause.

Beyond the bar and the tidal runnel farther in, the flat region I call the upper beach runs back to the shadeless bastion of the dunes. In summer this beach is rarely covered by the tides. Here lies a hot and pleasant odour of sand. I find myself an angle of shade slanting off from a mass of wreckage still embedded in a dune, take up a handful of the dry, bright sand, sift it slowly through my fingers, and note how the heat brings out the fine, sharp, stony smell of it. There is weed here, too, well buried in the dry sand — flotsam of last month's high, full-moon tides. In the shadowless glare, the topmost fronds and heart-shaped air sacs have ripened to an odd iodine orange and a blackish iodine brown. Overwhelmed thus by sand and heat, the aroma of this foliage has dissolved; only a shower will summon it again from these crisping, strangely coloured leaves.

Cool breath of eastern ocean, the aroma of beach vegetation in the sun, the hot, pungent exhalation of fine sand — these mingled are the midsummer savour of the beach.

Hyemeyohsts
Storm

SEVEN ARROWS

To Touch and Feel is to Experience. Many people live out their entire lives without ever really Touching or being Touched by anything. These people live within a world of mind and imagination that may move them sometimes to joy, tears, happiness or sorrow. But these people never really Touch. They do not live and become one with life.

Helen
Keller

THE STORY OF MY LIFE

What a joy it is
    to feel the soft, springy earth under my feet
  once more,
to follow grassy roads that lead to ferny brooks
  where I can bathe my fingers in a cataract of rippling
  notes,
or to clamber over a stone wall into green fields that
  tumble and roll and climb in riotous gladness!

Henry Beston

NORTHERN FARM

One aspect of the machine world which has not had sufficient attention is the relation of the machine age to the mystery of human joy. If there is one thing clear about the centuries dominated by the factory and the wheel, it is that although the machine can make everything from a spoon to a landing-craft, a natural joy in earthly living is something it never has and never will be able to manufacture. It has given us conveniences (often most uncomfortable) and comforts (often most inconvenient) but human happiness was never on its tray of wares. The historical result of the era has been an economic world so glutted with machine power that it is being shaken apart like a jerry-built factory, and a frustrate human world full of neurotic and ugly substitutes for joy.

Part of the confused violence of our time represents, I think, the unconscious search of man for his own natural happiness. He cannot live by bread alone and particularly not by sawdust bread. To speak in paradox, a sense of some joy in living is one of the most serious things in all the world.

Sigurd
Olson

REFLECTIONS FROM THE NORTH COUNTRY

Awareness is becoming acquainted with environment, no matter where one happens to be. Man
does not suddenly become aware or infused with
wonder; it is something we are born with. No child
need be told its secret; he keeps it until the influence
of gadgetry and the indifference of teen-age satiation
extinguish its intuitive joy.

Rachel
Carson

SENSE OF WONDER

I f I had influence with the good fairy who is supposed to preside over the christening of all children I should ask that her gift to each child in the world be a sense of wonder so indestructible that it would last throughout life, as an unfailing antidote against the boredom and disenchantments of later years, the sterile preoccupation with things that are artificial, the alienation from the sources of our strength.

If a child is to keep alive his inborn sense of wonder without any such gift from the fairies, he needs the companionship of at least one adult who can share it, rediscovering with him the joy, excitement and mystery of the world we live in. Parents often have a sense of inadequacy when confronted on the one hand with the eager, sensitive mind of a child and on the other with a world of complex physical nature, inhabited by a life so various and unfamiliar that it seems hopeless to reduce it to order and knowledge.

In a mood of self-defeat, they exclaim, "How can I possibly teach my child about nature — why, I don't even know one bird from another!"

I sincerely believe that for the child, and for the parent seeking to guide him, it is not half so important to *know* as to *feel*. If facts are the seeds that later produce knowledge and wisdom, then the emotions and the impressions of the senses are the fertile soil in which the seeds must grow. The years of early childhood are the time to prepare the soil. Once the emotions have been aroused — a sense of the beautiful, the excitement of the new and the unknown, a feeling of sympathy, pity, admiration or love — then we wish for knowledge about the object of our emotional response. Once found, it has lasting meaning. It is more important to pave the way for the child to want to know than to put him on a diet of facts he is not ready to assimilate.

Shel Silverstein

WHERE THE SIDEWALK ENDS

There is a place where the sidewalk ends
And before the street begins,
And there the grass grows soft and white,
And there the sun burns crimson bright,
And there the moon-bird rests from his flight
To cool in the peppermint wind.

Let us leave this place where the smoke blows black
And the dark street winds and bends.
Past the pits where the asphalt flowers grow
We shall walk with a walk that is measured and
    slow,
And watch where the chalk-white arrows go
To the place where the sidewalk ends.

Yes we'll walk with a walk that is measured and
    slow,
And we'll go where the chalk-white arrows go,
For the children, they mark, and the children, they
    know
The place where the sidewalk ends.

T.J. Walker

RED SALMON, BROWN BEAR

The fact remains that the people who profess to know about these things and to love them haven't the vaguest notion of how to see nature. They don't know where to find it, they don't know how to experience it, and if they demonstrate the existence of it they do so on a field trip which is more a social outing than a field trip. If anything, they do more damage to nature by their activity than they do if they never brought the kids out at all. The point is that people should find these things out for themselves. You shouldn't have to go to some expert to know that if you look here or there you'll find something. You're there — look! It's as simple as that.

Sigurd Olson

LISTENING POINT

While we are born with curiosity and wonder
and our early years full of the adventure
  they bring,
I know such inherent joys are often lost.
I also know that, being deep within us,
their latent glow can be fanned to flame again
by awareness and an open mind.

Kahlil Gibran

THE PROPHET

And forget not that the earth delights to feel your bare feet and the winds long to play with your hair.

Edward
Abbey

THE JOURNEY HOME

A couple of years ago I had a job. I worked for an outfit called Defenders of Fur Bearers (now known as Defenders of Wildlife). I was caretaker and head janitor of a 70,000-acre wildlife refuge in the vicinity of Aravaipa Canyon in southern Arizona. The Whittell Wildlife Preserve, as we called it, was a refuge for mountain lion, javelina, a few black bear, maybe a wolf or two, a herd of whitetail deer, and me, to name the principal fur bearers.

I was walking along Aravaipa Creek one afternoon when I noticed fresh mountain lion tracks leading ahead of me. Big tracks, the biggest lion tracks I've seen anywhere. Now I've lived most of my life in the Southwest, but I am sorry to admit that I had never seen a mountain lion in the wild. Naturally I was eager to get a glimpse of this one.

It was getting late in the day, the sun already down beyond the canyon wall, so I hurried along, hoping I might catch up to the lion and get one good look at him before I had to turn back and head home. But no matter how fast I walked and then jogged along, I couldn't seem to get any closer; those big tracks kept leading ahead of me, looking not five minutes old, but always disappearing around the next turn in the canyon.

Twilight settled in, visibility getting poor. I realized I'd have to call it quits. I stopped for a while, staring upstream into the gloom of the canyon. I could see the buzzards settling down for the evening in their favorite dead cottonwood. I heard the poor-wills and the spotted toads beginning to sing, but of that mountain lion I could neither hear nor see any living trace.

I turned around and started home. I'd walked maybe a mile when I thought I heard something odd behind me. I stopped and looked back — nothing; nothing but the canyon, the running water, the trees, the rocks, the willow thickets. I went on and soon I heard that noise again — the sound of footsteps.

I stopped. The noise stopped. Feeling a bit uncomfortable now — it was getting dark — with all the ancient superstitions of the night starting to crawl from the crannies of my soul, I looked back again.

And this time I saw him. About fifty yards behind me, poised on a sand bar, one front paw still lifted and waiting, stood this big cat, looking straight at me. I could see the gleam of the twilight in his eyes. I was startled as always by how small a cougar's head seems but how long and lean and powerful the body really is. To me, at that moment, he looked like the biggest cat in the world. He looked dangerous. Now I know very well that mountain lions are supposed almost never to attack human beings. I knew there was nothing to fear — but I couldn't help thinking maybe this lion is different from the others. Maybe he knows we're in a wildlife preserve, where lions can get away with anything. I was not unarmed; I had my Swiss army knife in my pocket with the built-in can opener, the corkscrew, the two-inch folding blade, the screwdriver. Rationally there was nothing to fear; all the same I felt fear.

And something else too: I felt what I always feel when I meet a large animal face to face in the wild: I felt a kind of affection and the crazy desire to communicate, to make some kind of emotional, even physical contact with the animal. After we'd stared at each other for maybe five seconds — it seemed at the time like five minutes — I held out one hand and took a step toward the big cat and said something ridiculous like, "Here, kitty, kitty." The cat paused there on three legs, one paw up as if he wanted to shake hands. But he didn't respond to my advance.

I took a second step toward the lion. Again the lion remained still, not moving a muscle, not blinking an eye. And I stopped and thought again and this time I understood that however the big cat might secretly feel, I myself was not quite ready to shake hands with a mountain lion. Maybe someday. But not yet. I retreated.

I turned and walked homeward again, pausing every few steps to look back over my shoulder. The cat had lowered his front paw but did not follow me. The last I saw of him, from the next bend of the canyon, he was still in the same place, watching me go. I hurried on through the evening, stopping now and then to look and listen, but if that cat followed me any further I could detect no sight or sound of it.

I haven't seen a mountain lion since that evening, but the experience remains shining in my memory. I want my children to have the opportunity for that kind of experience. I want my friends to have it. I want even our enemies to have it — they need it most. And someday, possibly, one of our children's children will discover how to get close enough to that mountain lion to shake paws with it, to embrace and caress it, maybe even teach it something, and to learn what the lion has to teach us.

Alan
Gussow

A SENSE OF PLACE

There is a great deal of talk these days about saving the environment. We must, for the environment sustains our bodies. But as humans we also require support for our spirits, and this is what certain kinds of places provide. The catalyst that converts any physical location — any environment if you will — into a place, is the process of experiencing deeply. A place is a piece of the whole environment that has been claimed by feelings. Viewed simply as a life-support system, the earth is an environment. Viewed as a resource that sustains our humanity, the earth is a collection of places. We never speak, for example, of an environment we have known; it is always places we have known — and recall. We are homesick for places, we are reminded of places, it is the sounds and smells and sights of places which haunt us and against which we often measure our present.

Joseph Wood Krutch

THE DESERT YEAR

A "tour" is like a cocktail party. One "meets" everybody and knows no one. I doubt that what is ordinarily called "travel" really does broaden the mind any more than a cocktail party cultivates the soul. Perhaps the old-fashioned tourist who used to check off items in his Baedeker lest he forget that he had seen them was not legitimately so much a figure of fun as he was commonly made. At best, more sophisticated travelers usually know only the fact that they have seen something, not anything worth keeping which they got from the sight itself. Chartres is where the lunch was good; Lake Leman where we couldn't get a porter. To have lived in three places, perhaps really to have lived in only one, is better than to have seen a hundred. I am a part, said Ulysses, of all that I have known — not of all that I have visited or "viewed."

In defense of cocktail parties it is commonly said

that they are not ends in themselves but only, more or less frankly, occasions on which people offer themselves for inspection by their fellows. Young men and young women attend in order, as they say, "to look 'em over"; older people in order, as they more sedately put it, on the chance of meeting someone whose acquaintance they would like to cultivate. Something of the same sort is the most that can be said in defense of the tour. Of some spot of earth one may feel that one would like it if one could really see or really know it.

Here, one may say, I should like to stay for a month, or a year, or a decade. It could give something to me and I, perhaps, something to it — if only some sort of love and understanding. More rarely — perhaps only once, perhaps two or three times — one experiences something more like love at first sight. The desire to stay, to enter in, is not a whim or a notion but a passion. *Verweile doch, du bist so schön!* If I do not somehow possess this, if I never learn what it was that called out, what it was that was being offered, I shall feel all my life that I have missed something intended for me. If I do not, for a time at least, live here I shall not have lived as fully as I had the capacity to live.

Dag Hammarskjöld

MARKINGS

S o rests the sky against the earth. The dark still tarn in the lap of the forest. As a husband embraces his wife's body in faithful tenderness, so the bare ground and trees are embraced by the still, high, light of the morning.

I feel an ache of longing to share in this embrace, to be united and absorbed. A longing like carnal desire, but directed towards earth, water, sky, and returned by the whispers of the trees, the fragrance of the soil, the caresses of the wind, the embrace of water and light. Content? No, no, no — but refreshed, rested — while waiting.

John
Burroughs

I am in love with this world. I have nestled lovingly
in it. I have climbed its mountains, roamed its
forests, sailed its waters, crossed its deserts, felt the
sting of its frosts, the oppression of its heats, the
drench of its rains, the fury of its winds, and always
have beauty and joy waited upon my goings and
comings.

Wallace Stegner

SOUND OF MOUNTAIN WATER

I gave my heart to the mountains the minute I stood beside this river with its spray in my face and watched it thunder into foam, smooth to green glass over sunken rocks, shatter to foam again . . .

It was rare and comforting to waken late and hear the undiminished shouting of the water in the night. And at sunup it was still there, powerful and incessant, with the slant sun tangled in its rainbow spray, the grass blue with wetness, and the air heady as ether and scented with campfire smoke.

By such a river it is impossible to believe that one will ever be tired or old. Every sense applauds it. Taste it, feel its chill on the teeth: it is purity absolute. Watch its racing current, its steady renewal of force: it is transient and eternal. And listen again to its sounds: get far enough away so that the noise of falling tons of water does not stun the ears, and hear how much is going on underneath — a whole symphony of smaller sounds, hiss and splash and gurgle, the small talk of side channels, the whisper of blown and scattered spray gathering itself and beginning to flow again, secret and irresistible, among the wet rocks.

John Muir

MY FIRST SUMMER IN THE SIERRA

How deep our sleep last night in the mountain's heart, beneath the trees and stars, hushed by solemn-sounding waterfalls and many small soothing voices in sweet accord whispering peace!

And our first pure mountain day, warm, calm, cloudless, — how immeasurable it seems, how serenely wild! I can scarcely remember its beginning. Along the river, over the hills, in the ground, in the sky, spring work is going on with joyful enthusiasm, new life, new beauty, unfolding, unrolling in glorious exuberant extravagance, — new birds in their nests, new winged creatures in the air, and new leaves, new flowers, spreading, shining, rejoicing everywhere.

Henry David Thoreau

WALDEN

We need the tonic of wildness —
　　to wade sometimes in marshes
where the bittern and the meadow-hen lurk,
and hear the booming of the snipe;
to smell the whispering sedge where only some
　　wilder and more solitary fowl builds her nest,
and the mink crawls with its belly close to the ground.
At the same time that we are earnest to explore
　　and learn all things,
we require that all things be mysterious and
　　unexplorable,
that land and sea be infinitely wild,
unsurveyed and unfathomed by us because
　　unfathomable.
We can never have enough of nature.
We must be refreshed by the sight of inexhaustible
　　vigor,
vast and titantic features,

the sea-coast with its wrecks,
the wilderness with its living and its decaying trees,
the thunder-cloud,
and the rain which lasts three weeks
   and produces freshets.
We need to witness our own limits transgressed,
and some life pasturing freely
   where we never wander.

Aldo Leopold

A SAND COUNTY ALMANAC

Man always kills the things he loves, and so we the pioneers have killed our wilderness. Some say we had to. Be that as it may, I am glad I shall never be young without wild country to be young in. Of what avail are forty freedoms without a blank spot on the map?

Edward
Abbey

One final paragraph of advice: Do not burn yourselves out. Be as I am — a reluctant enthusiast . . . a part-time crusader, a half-hearted fanatic. Save the other half of yourselves and your lives for pleasure and adventure. It is not enough to fight for the land; it is even more important to enjoy it. While you can. While it's still here. So get out there and hunt and fish and mess around with your friends, ramble out yonder and explore the forests, encounter the grizz, climb the mountains, bag the peaks, run the rivers, breathe deep of that yet sweet and lucid air, sit quietly for a while and contemplate the precious stillness, that lovely, mysterious and awesome space. Enjoy yourselves, keep your brain in your head and your head firmly attached to the body, the body active and alive, and I promise you this much: I promise you this one sweet victory over our enemies, over those deskbound people with their hearts in a safe deposit box and their eyes hypnotized by desk calculators. I promise you this: you will outlive the bastards.

Li Po

Since water still flows, though we cut it with
swords
And sorrow returns, though we drown it with wine,
Since the world can in no way answer to our craving,
I will loosen my hair tomorrow and take to a fishing
boat.

EARTH WISDOM

EARTH WISDOM

Steve Van Matre

WE TRAVEL THROUGH THE VOIDS OF SPACE ON
A SMALL, SELF-CONTAINED LIFE VESSEL powered
by the energy of the stars. It is a marvelous ship of life,
probably one of the most wondrous and rare in the
universe. Yet in our human-centered ignorance and
arrogance we have tried to create a different world, to
create an existence separate from our fellow passengers,
to confine the other species that share the vessel with us
to smaller and smaller compartments while we command
more and more space for our burgeoning numbers and
desires.

The earth is in danger of becoming a monstrous slave
ship sailing on the cosmic tides of the Milky Way. To
support our continually expanding population of human
passengers we are systematically destroying or enslaving
much of the other life of the ship we sail upon. And we
have used the fossil sunlight and water discovered in
various holds of the ship to support artificial
compartments where a relatively small number of us live
in amazing luxury. In fact, compared to the majority of

the ship's human passengers most of us in western societies live in these synthetic, unnatural settings like swollen grubs feeding off of the energy-rich micro-environments we have created, all the while spewing forth our resulting disorder and poisonous wastes to contaminate other areas of the vessel.

It gets worse. As elite passengers, we are also creating a culture based upon "synathetics" where acceptance and beauty is often determined by the amount of fossil energy invested, and our actions have set this energy-rich fantasy as the standard for the world. It is said that Disney's new EPCOT Center may become the premier tourist attraction on earth. If so, all who enter should be forewarned to skip Future World. This highly polished, stainless steel and plasticized spectacle is not what it claims to be. It is the Environmental Propaganda Center Of Tomorrow, and that vision of the future is hazardous to the health of our planet. Tragically, such a portrayal could have been predicted, for our high-energy addiction has blinded us, stunting our growth, causing us to turn inward, losing sight of the realities of our life here. Most of us don't see the earth as it really is. We have lived too long in our energy-rich urban colonies. We react in amazement when told that there are more sharks here than people, for we have come to see the earth as people and cities and highways and hotels — a continually growing progression of synthetic attractions.

Cousteau suggested that "gigantism" was a primary factor in the decline of the civilization on Easter Island, for in the midst of widespread deprivation and starvation the islanders were still tying up significant resources in carving colossal ancestor statues out of the mountain rock. It was as if they couldn't control the system they had created. Their religious and social stratification had actually imprisoned them, trapped them in a system that continued turning out gargantuan products on one end even when the other end had no base of support left — no food, no fuel, no stamina for the continued growth expected. So what does Cousteau's story have to do with us today? Are not our modern skyscrapers our present statues, in this case gigantic phallic symbols thrust above our skylines proclaiming our conquest of the earth even as most of our species continues to struggle for survival? Is not our contemporary view of progress and growth just as distorted as that of those islanders centuries ago?

People should not spend their entire lives in a skyscrapered city, for in the midst of those artificial canyons they will likely forget who and where they are. If people are stopped on the street of a major city today and asked what supports the life of the earth, they will probably reply that their city does. Isn't it strange that people can name the trees along the sidewalk but don't understand how sunlight supports the life of earth? Perhaps we have entrusted an understanding of our planet and its problems to the wrong people: to those who spend their time primarily inventorying the natural world, to those who pass out freeze-dried frogs at the science teachers' conventions, to those who claim that trees cause pollution. In fact, those who explain the workings of earth best sound more like poets than teachers. Consider the words of Collins or Edberg with which we begin this portion of THE EARTH SPEAKS. Perhaps we should hire the poets instead of the biologists to write our science textbooks! Undoubtedly, we must simplify our messages and express them in ways that assure more lasting effects. We have included several of our favorite approaches in this section: the subdued imagery of a Carson and an Olson, the earthy strength of a Whitman, the fun facts used by a Platt, and the drama and clarity provided by an Eiseley.

A state department of conservation in the Midwest conducted a survey on how people liked to get in touch with nature, and to their surprise the overwhelming majority said they liked nature best on television! And why not? Many who attend our live nature programs yearn for M and M's (magic and meaning) and get N and N's (names and numbers) instead. Is it any wonder then that they turn to something that can simplify and dramatize the object of their interest? A story making the rounds a few years ago illustrates the point. Two people were given the same task — to explain some essential understandings about astronomy to a university class. One was an actor, the other an astronomer. And which class do you suppose retained the points longer and rated the experience as the more enjoyable? Score one for good communication. What a strange dilemma we face. The leaders of our countries often appear to have little or no real understanding of how life functions here, while the leaders of programs that might redress the problem frequently appear to be hobbyists instead of educators. We are all too often led by the environmentally illiterate and served by the educationally disinterested. This is not to ignore the many real and significant contributions made daily by a host of those laboring in this field, often with little or no support, but overall it has obviously not been enough. And many have gone astray. We urgently need to refocus. We must cut through the natural history recitations and start helping people understand the big picture ecological concepts, what these understandings mean for their own lives, and how we must all begin to change our lifestyles in order to live more harmoniously with the earth.

The unnatural world we have created here is surely doomed. As the ship's stores of fossil fuel and water are depleted, our fungus-like, energy-bloated urban colonies will shrink and wither. People will return to the land to create more labor-intensive, decentralized lifestyles. To prepare for the future we should study the past, relearn (and improve upon while we can) ways of living on minimal amounts of fossil fuel and water. Now is the time to get ready. We should seek out those who have demonstrated a wisdom nurtured by close contact with the earth and listen to their words. The simple, eloquent messages of Chief Seattle and Gary Snyder may be widely separated in time but not in inner truth. They have the solid ring of being sound. Such people know that genuine wisdom lies not in understanding but in caring about what you understand. A skilled man can build a skyscraper, but only a wise man can help us judge how best to use those skills.

Imagine for a moment that you are sitting right now in an intergalactic council meeting listening to a speaker describe a ship with which they have made radio contact in a remote galaxy called the Milky Way:

"Fellow council members, we have been in touch with this life vessel for over a month now and during that time we have been informed about the following conditions: First, over fifteen million of this ship's human passengers are dying each year of starvation and nutrition-related disease; second, some environmental scientists on board report that the human life on this ship is also destroying other kinds of life, their fellow passengers, at the rate of one species per day; third, tens of thousands of the human passengers die each day of environmentally induced stress and disease; fourth, the life support systems on board have been severely disrupted by the introduction of vast quantities of synthetically produced substances which now threaten the well-being of large numbers of passengers; fifth, armed conflict claims the lives of millions each year as the human passengers fight among themselves to maintain control over the dwindling food and fuel supplies on board."

Is there any doubt that as a member of such a council meeting you would conclude that "that ship is in trouble"? You would be right. It is. Perhaps the problem is not that we didn't work well enough together, but that we worked too well. In fact, maybe if we hadn't worked so well together, we wouldn't be destroying the earth so rapidly. For the future, perhaps our motto should become: love the earth first and its people second. Or as Rolf Edberg put it: "What has gone wrong, probably, is that we have failed to see ourselves as part of a large and indivisible whole . . . we have failed to understand that the earth does not belong to us, but we to the earth."

Indian Proverb

The frog does not drink up
the pond in which he lives.

Lawrence Collins

ONLY A LITTLE PLANET

The planet you're standing on
looking out at the stars
is the earth, the third planet from the sun

and the mildest
and softest
of the nine. . . .

If you can stop, and let yourself look,
let your eyes do
what they do best,
stop
and let yourself see and see
that everything is doing things
to you
as you do things to everything.

Then you know
that although it is only a little planet
it is hugely beautiful
and surely the finest place in the world
to be.

So watch it, look at it
see what it's like
to walk around on it.

It's small but it's beautiful
it's small but it's fine
like a rainbow,

like a bubble.

Lewis Thomas

THE LIVES OF A CELL

Viewed from the distance of the moon, the astonishing thing about the earth, catching the breath, is that it is alive. The photographs show the dry, pounded surface of the moon in the foreground, dead as an old bone. Aloft, floating free beneath the moist, gleaming membrane of bright blue sky, is the rising earth, the only exuberant thing in this part of the cosmos. If you could look long enough, you would see the swirling of the great drifts of white cloud, covering and uncovering the half-hidden masses of land. If you had been looking for a very long, geologic time, you could have seen the continents themselves in motion, drifting apart on their crustal plates, held afloat by the fire beneath. It has the organized, self-contained look of a live creature, full of information, marvelously skilled in handling the sun.

It takes a membrane to make sense out of disorder

in biology. You have to be able to catch energy and hold it, storing precisely the needed amount and releasing it in measured shares. A cell does this, and so do the organelles inside. Each assemblage is poised in the flow of solar energy, tapping off energy from metabolic surrogates of the sun. To stay alive, you have to be able to hold out against equilibrium, maintain imbalance, bank against entropy, and you can only transact this business with membranes in our kind of world.

When the earth came alive it began constructing its own membrane, for the general purpose of editing the sun . . .

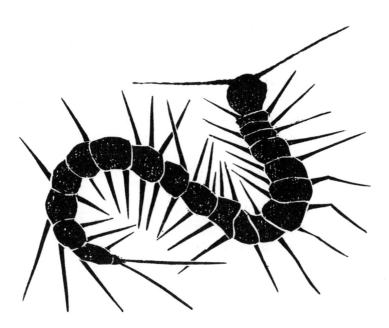

Lawrence Collins

ONLY A LITTLE PLANET

Every particle of every thing
rock, water, flower, human
has been in the same place flaming
in the heart of our ancient sun
before the earth
came flying out of it.

The irises in your eyes
the tissue of roses

the slow giant rocks in mountain hearts

were all born flaming
locked in the sun as it drifted
like a light on dark water.

A. Rolf
Edberg

ON THE SHRED OF A CLOUD

S tand and fill your lungs with air. With every
breath you inhale a thousand billion billion
atoms. A few million billion of them are long-living
argon atoms that are exhaled within the second and
dispersed with the winds. Time mixes them and has
been mixing them for a long time. Some of them may
have visited Buddha or Caesar, or even earlier paid a
call on the man from Makapan.

Rachel
Carson

THE EDGE OF THE SEA

Once this rocky coast beneath me was a plain of
sand; then the sea rose and found a new shore line.
And again in some shadowy future the surf will have
ground these rocks to sand and will have returned the
coast to its earlier state. And so in my mind's eye
these coastal forms merge and blend in a shifting,
kaleidoscopic pattern in which there is no finality, no
ultimate and fixed reality — earth becoming fluid as
the sea itself.

Walt Whitman

"UNSEEN BUDS"

Unseen buds, infinite, hidden well,
　Under the snow and ice, under the darkness, in
every square or cubic inch,
Germinal, exquisite, in delicate lace, microscopic,
unborn,
Like babes in wombs, latent, folded, compact,
sleeping;
Billions of billions, and trillions of trillions of them
waiting,
(On earth and in the sea — the universe —
the stars there in the heavens,)
Urging slowly, surely forward, forming endless,
And waiting ever more, forever more behind.

Rutherford
Platt

THE GREAT AMERICAN FOREST

Food in the human menu is hardly recognized as packaged sunlight, but that is exactly what it is. The art of packaging sunlight was originally discovered by plants in the sea, and seaweeds carried the formula for photosynthesis to the water's edge. There they delivered it to ferns and mosses, which in turn bequeathed it to trees.

Growing in the sunlight, trees could make full use of photosynthesis; in fact, their energy factory worked so well that packaged sunlight was not only incorporated into food but into wood, as we have seen. Then wood, in turn, increased the production of packaged sunlight by lifting green needles and leaves high off the ground into more winds, bringing more oxygen and giving more exposure to sunlight. These towering arrangements led to the grand climax of forests ...

At first glance, a leaf may look as thin as paper; actually it is a spreading one-story factory with ample room between floor and ceiling for sunlight-packaging machinery. The standard leaf is designed for utility to present a broad surface to the sunlight. A mature maple tree spreads several hundred thousand leaves with a surface of some two thousand square yards (about half an acre) of chlorophyll.

A square yard of leaf surface in full operation packs about a gram of carbohydrate per hour. This may seem to be a small amount; a gram weighs about as much as the common straight pin. But food production of that half acre of chlorophyll mounts with each hour of every day. There are no Sunday and holiday shutdowns. Photosynthesis does not require a bright sunny day, it works even better when the sky is overcast. Operating an average of ten hours a day during June, July and August, each square yard of maple leaf surface packs a pound and a half of carbohydrate. The seasonal production by the leaves of a single maple tree can total 3,630 pounds of packaged sunlight!

Edwin Way Teale

DUNE BOY,
THE EARLY YEARS OF A NATURALIST

For a great tree death comes as a gradual transformation. Its vitality ebbs slowly. Even when life has abandoned it entirely it remains a majestic thing. On some hilltop a dead tree may dominate the landscape for miles around. Alone among living things it retains its character and dignity after death. Plants wither; animals disintegrate. But a dead tree may be as arresting, as filled with personality, in death as it is in life. Even in its final moments, when the massive trunk lies prone and it has moldered into a ridge covered with mosses and fungi, it arrives at a fitting and noble end. It enriches and refreshes the earth. And later, as part of other green and growing things, it rises again.

Robert Francis

"EARTHWORM"

My spading fork turning the earth turns
This fellow out — without touching him this
time.
Robbed of all resistance to his progress
He squirms awhile in the too-easy air
Before an ancient and implicit purpose
Starts him traveling in one direction
Reaching out, contracting, reaching out,
Contracting — a clean and glistening earth-pink.
He has turned more earth than I have with my fork.
He has lifted more earth than all men have or will.
Breaking the earth in spring men break his body.
And it is broken in the beaks of birds.
He has become and will again become
The flying and singing of birds. Yet another spring
I shall find him working noiselessly in the earth.
When I am earth again he will be there.

Sigurd Olson

"THE SOUND OF RAIN"

Last night in my tent I listened to the rain. At first it came down gently, then in a steady drumming downpour, and I lay there wondering when I would begin to feel the first rivulets creeping beneath my sleeping-bag. The deluge continued, but there were no exploring trickles, no mist through the roof of balloon silk. The tent, on the little rise with its thick cushion of bearberry, had perfect drainage all around, and the ropes were tied to two good trees. The gale could blow now and the rain come down, but I would be safe and dry the rest of the night. I settled down luxuriously to enjoy a sound I had known on countless campsites in the wilderness.

Like all woodsmen, I had planned for the morning, had tucked a roll of dry birchbark and a few slivers of pine under one end of the canoe. My packs were in one corner of the tent, the ax handy just in case something snapped during the night. The canoe was snubbed to a rock well up from the shore.

The wind came up and the tent swayed, but the ropes held; in the rain they grew taut as fiddle strings and the tent more waterproof with each new assault. A branch swished close and two trees rubbed against each other. The woods were full of sounds, creakings and groanings, with branches dropping from the trees.

How much good the rain would do, how fresh the water in every stream, how flowers would pop with the sun, the linnaea, the anemones, the dogwood and everything else along the trails. The ferns on the rocks would begin to grow again, and the silvery caribou moss would be soft and resilient with just a tinge of green. The dry and brittle lichens along the cliffs would turn from black to velvet green. Mushrooms and toadstools would suddenly emerge from every dead log, and the dusty humus would bring forth growths that had been waiting for this very hour, for no rain had fallen in a month.

The coming of the rain soothed a longing within me for moisture and lushness after the long-continued drought. As I lay there, I too seemed to expand and grow, became part of the lushness and the rain itself and of all the thirsty life about me. This is one of the reasons I like to hear the rain come down on a tent. I am close to it then, as close as one can be without actually being in it. I have slept in many primitive shelters, under overhanging cliffs, in lean-tos made of spruce boughs and birchbark, in little cabins roofed with poles and sod. I have slept under canoes and boats and under the spreading branches of pines and balsams, but none of these places gives me quite the feeling I get when sleeping in a tent.

The drops are muffled by the cloth, none of the staccato drumming there is under a hard roof. Once I slept in a cabin with a tin roof and listened to a chorus that night that was too violent to enjoy, a mechanical sound as though a thousand drums had broken into a rolling crescendo all at once.

Not long ago I met an old friend, C.K. Leith, one of the world's most famous geologists. He had been a professor of mine, and for a time I had worked under him on the Wisconsin Geological Survey. After his retirement, he had served as a consultant to the government, using his great knowledge of the world's minerals to guide exploration and development.

We sat in the Cosmos Club one rainy afternoon talking about the old days, the days in the bush when he was a legend of endurance and fortitude, of the treks he had made into the far north that even today are contemplated with awe and wonderment by hardened prospectors. He was eighty-two when I talked to him last, but still as straight and energetic as ever. Suddenly he was quiet, a faraway look came into his eyes as he sat watching the rain spatter down into the courtyard.

"Do you know where I'd like to be right now?" he said finally. "In my old tent somewhere, safe and dry with nothing to do but listen to the rain come down."

He smiled and I knew he was cruising the back country of the Canadian Shield, down its brawling rivers, across its stormy lakes, knowing again the feeling of distance and space, the sense of the old wilderness.

"As you get older," he said, "and more involved with world affairs, you lose that life, but those were the good old days for me."

When I heard of his passing, I knew that somewhere back in the bush he was listening to the rain come down and that he had found again the life he loved.

In the woods of Listening Point, the drops soak into the ground as they should, stopped by an intricate baffle system of leaves and pine needles, small sticks and bits of bark, the partly decayed vegetation just underneath, and finally the humus itself, rich, black, and absorbent, the accumulation of ten thousand years. Here in the north it takes over a thousand years to form a single inch of it, and if the glacier receded from seven to ten thousand years ago, the humus on the point has taken just that long to form.

Below the humus is the mineral rock soil, the result not only of the grinding of glacial ice but the gradual breakdown of the granite and schist and greenstone by the frost and rain, the action of the acids of countless roots, the burrowing of hordes of insects and worms and beetles. This layer rests upon the native ledge, but by the time the rain reaches it, it has slowed and soaks into it without loss. There are no rivulets except where the rock is bare, no erosion or run-off to the lake. All that falls stays there and moves into the water table of the area to be held in reserve.

It was good to lie in the tent knowing the rain was replenishing the water supply, that none of it was being lost except where it ran off the smooth rocks, that even between them, in every cleft and crevice where there was any accumulation of humus at all, it would be held for months to come.

Loren Eiseley

"HOW FLOWERS CHANGED THE WORLD"

If it had been possible to observe the Earth from the far side of the solar system over the long course of geological epochs, the watchers might have been able to discern a subtle change in the light emanating from our planet. That world of long ago would, like the red deserts of Mars, have reflected light from vast drifts of stone and gravel, the sands of wandering wastes, the blackness of naked basalt, the yellow dust of endlessly moving storms. Only the ceaseless marching of the clouds and the intermittent flashes from the restless surface of the sea would have told a different story, but still essentially a barren one. Then, as the millennia rolled away and age followed age, a new and greener light would, by degrees, have come to twinkle across those endless miles.

This is the only difference those far watchers, by the use of subtle instruments, might have perceived in the whole history of the planet Earth. Yet that slowly growing green twinkle would have contained the epic march of life from the tidal oozes upward across the raw and unclothed continents. Out of the vast chemical bath of the sea — not from the deeps, but from the element-rich, light-exposed platforms of the continental shelves — wandering fingers of green had crept upward along the meanderings of river systems and fringed the gravels of forgotten lakes.

In those first ages plants clung of necessity to swamps and watercourses. Their reproductive processes demanded direct access to water. Beyond the primitive ferns and mosses that enclosed the borders of swamps and streams the rocks still lay vast and bare, the winds still swirled the dust of a naked planet. The grass cover that holds our world secure in place was still millions of years in the future. The green marchers had gained a soggy foothold upon the land, but that was all. They did not reproduce by seeds but by microscopic swimming sperm that had to wriggle their way through water to fertilize the female cell. Such plants in their higher forms had clever adaptations for the use of rain water in their sexual phases, and survived with increasing success in a wetland environment. They now seem part of man's normal environment. The truth is, however, that there is nothing very "normal" about nature. Once upon a time there were no flowers at all.

A little while ago — about one hundred million years, as the geologist estimates time in the history of our four-billion-year-old planet — flowers were not to be found anywhere on the five continents. Wherever one might have looked, from the poles to the equator, one would have seen only the cold dark monotonous green of a world whose plant life possessed no other color.

Somewhere, just a short time before the close of the Age of Reptiles, there occurred a soundless, violent explosion. It lasted millions of years, but it was an explosion, nevertheless. It marked the emergence of the angiosperms — the flowering plants. Even the great evolutionist, Charles Darwin, called them "an abominable mystery," because they appeared so suddenly and spread so fast.

Flowers changed the face of the planet. Without them, the world we know — even man himself — would never have existed. Francis Thompson, the English poet, once wrote that one could not pluck a flower without troubling a star. Intuitively he had sensed like a naturalist the enormous interlinked complexity of life. Today we know that the appearance of the flowers contained also the equally mystifying emergence of man.

If we were to go back into the Age of Reptiles, its drowned swamps and birdless forests would reveal to us a warmer but, on the whole, a sleepier world than that of today. Here and there, it is true, the serpent heads of bottom-feeding dinosaurs might be upreared in suspicion of their huge flesh-eating compatriots. Tyrannosaurs, enormous bipedal caricatures of men, would stalk mindlessly across the sites of future cities and go their slow way down into the dark of geologic time.

In all that world of living things nothing saw save with the intense concentration of the hunt, nothing moved except with the grave sleepwalking intentness of the instinct-driven brain. Judged by modern standards, it was a world in slow motion, a cold-blooded world whose occupants were most active at noonday but torpid on chill nights, their brains damped by a slower metabolism than any known to even the most primitive of warm-blooded animals today.

A high metabolic rate and the maintenance of a constant body temperature are supreme achievements in the evolution of life. They enable an animal to escape, within broad limits, from the overheating or the chilling of its immediate surroundings, and at the same time to maintain a peak mental efficiency. Creatures without a high metabolic rate are slaves to weather. Insects in the first frosts of autumn all run down like little clocks. Yet if you pick one up and breathe warmly upon it, it will begin to move about once more.

In a sheltered spot such creatures may sleep away the winter, but they are hopelessly immobilized. Though a few warm-blooded mammals, such as the woodchuck of our day, have evolved a way of reducing their metabolic rate in order to undergo winter hibernation, it is a survival mechanism with drawbacks, for it leaves the animal helplessly exposed if enemies discover him during his period of suspended animation. Thus bear or woodchuck, big animal or small, must seek, in this time of descending sleep, a safe refuge in some hidden den or burrow. Hibernation is, therefore, primarily a winter refuge of small, easily concealed animals rather than of large ones.

A high metabolic rate, however, means a heavy intake of energy in order to sustain body warmth and efficiency. It is for this reason that even some of these later warm-blooded mammals existing in our day have learned to descend into a slower, unconscious rate of living during the winter months when food may be difficult to obtain. On a slightly higher plane they are following the procedure of the cold-blooded frog sleeping in the mud at the bottom of a frozen pond.

The agile brain of the warm-blooded birds and mammals demands a high oxygen consumption and food in concentrated forms, or the creatures cannot long sustain themselves. It was the rise of the flowering plants that provided that energy and changed the nature of the living world. Their appearance parallels in a quite surprising manner the rise of the birds and mammals.

Slowly, toward the dawn of the Age of Reptiles, something over two hundred and fifty million years ago, the little naked sperm cells wriggling their way through dew and raindrops had given way to a kind of pollen carried by the wind. Our present-day pine forests represent plants of a pollen-disseminating variety. Once fertilization was no longer dependent on exterior water, the march over drier regions could be extended. Instead of spores simple primitive seeds carrying some nourishment for the young plant had developed, but true flowers were still scores of millions of years away. After a long period of hesitant evolutionary groping, they exploded upon the world with truly revolutionary violence.

The event occurred in Cretaceous times in the close

of the Age of Reptiles. Before the coming of the flowering plants our own ancestral stock, the warm-blooded mammals, consisted of a few mousy little creatures hidden in trees and underbrush. A few lizard-like birds with carnivorous teeth flapped awkwardly on ill-aimed flights among archaic shrubbery. None of these insignificant creatures gave evidence of any remarkable talents. The mammals in particular had been around for some millions of years, but had remained well lost in the shadow of the mighty reptiles. Truth to tell, man was still, like the genie in the bottle, encased in the body of a creature about the size of a rat.

As for the birds, their reptilian cousins the Pterodactyls, flew farther and better. There was just one thing about the birds that paralleled the physiology of the mammals. They, too, had evolved warm blood and its accompanying temperature control. Nevertheless, if one had been seen stripped of his feathers, he would still have seemed a slightly uncanny and unsightly lizard.

Neither the birds nor the mammals, however, were quite what they seemed. They were waiting for the Age of Flowers. They were waiting for what flowers, and with them the true encased seed, would bring. Fish-eating, gigantic leather-winged reptiles, twenty-eight feet from wing tip to wing tip, hovered over the coasts that one day would be swarming with gulls.

Inland the monotonous green of the pine and spruce forest with their primitive wooden cone flowers stretched everywhere. No grass hindered the fall of the naked seeds to earth. Great sequoias towered to the skies. The world of that time has a certain appeal but it is a giant's world, a world moving slowly like the reptiles who stalked magnificently among the boles of its trees.

The trees themselves are ancient, slow-growing and immense, like the redwood groves that have survived to our day on the California coast. All is stiff, formal, upright and green, monotonously green. There is no grass as yet; there are no wide plains rolling in the sun, no tiny daisies dotting the meadows underfoot. There is little versatility about this scene; it is, in truth, a giant's world.

A few nights ago it was brought home vividly to me that the world has changed since that far epoch. I was awakened out of sleep by an unknown sound in my living room. Not a small sound — not a creaking timber or a mouse's scurry — but a sharp, rending explosion as though an unwary foot had been put down upon a wine glass. I had come instantly out of sleep and lay tense, unbreathing. I listened for another step. There was none.

Unable to stand the suspense any longer, I turned on the light and passed from room to room glancing uneasily behind chairs and into closets. Nothing seemed disturbed, and I stood puzzled in the center of the living room floor. Then a small button-shaped object upon the rug caught my eye. It was hard and polished and glistening. Scattered over the length of the room were several more shining up at me like wary little eyes. A pine cone that had been lying in a dish had been blown the length of the coffee table. The dish itself could hardly have been the source of the explosion. Beside it I found two ribbon-like strips of a velvety-green. I tried to place the two strips together to make a pod. They twisted resolutely away from each other and would no longer fit. I relaxed in a chair, then, for I had reached a solution of the midnight disturbance. The twisted strips were wistaria pods that I had brought in a day or two previously and placed in the dish. They had chosen midnight to explode and distribute their multiplying fund of life down the length of the room. A plant, a fixed, rooted thing, immobilized in a single spot, had devised a way of propelling its offspring across open space. Immediately there passed before my eyes the million airy troopers of the milkweed pod and the clutching hooks of the sandburs. Seeds on the coyote's tail, seeds on the hunter's coat, thistledown mounting on the winds — all were somehow triumphing over life's limitations. Yet the ability to do this had not been with them at the beginning. It was the product of endless effort and experiment.

The seeds on my carpet were not going to lie stiffly where they had dropped like their antiquated cousins, the naked seeds on the pine-cone scales. They were travelers. Struck by the thought, I went out next day and collected several other varieties. I line them up now in a row on my desk — so many little capsules of life, winged, hooked or spiked. Every one is an angiosperm, a product of the true flowering plants. Contained in these little boxes is the secret of that far-off Cretaceous explosion of a hundred million years ago that changed the face of the planet. And somewhere in here, I think, as I poke seriously at one particularly resistant seedcase of a wild grass, was once man himself.

W hen the first simple flower bloomed on some raw upland late in the Dinosaur Age, it was wind pollinated, just like its early pine-cone relatives. It was a very inconspicuous flower because it had not yet evolved the idea of using the surer attraction of birds and insects to achieve the transportation of pollen. It sowed its own pollen and received the pollen of other flowers by the simple vagaries of the wind. Many plants in regions where insect life is scant still follow this principle today. Nevertheless, the true flower — and the seed that it produced — was a profound innovation in the world of life.

In a way, this event parallels, in the plant world, what happened among animals. Consider the relative chance for survival of the exteriorly deposited egg of a fish in contrast with the fertilized egg of a mammal, carefully retained for months in the mother's body until the young animal (or human being) is developed to a point where it may survive. The biological wastage is less — and so it is with the flowering plants. The primitive spore, a single cell fertilized in the beginning by a swimming sperm, did not promote rapid distribution, and the young plant, moreover, had to struggle up from nothing. No one had left it any food except what it could get by its own unaided efforts.

By contrast, the true flowering plants (angiosperm itself means "encased seed") grew a seed in the heart of a flower, a seed whose development was initiated by a fertilizing pollen grain independent of outside moisture. But the seed, unlike the developing spore, is already a fully equipped *embryonic plant* packed in a little enclosed box stuffed full of nutritious food. Moreover, by featherdown attachments, as in dandelion or milkweed seed, it can be wafted upward on gusts and ride the wind for miles; or with hooks it can cling to a bear's or a rabbit's hide; or like some of the berries, it can be covered with a juicy, attractive fruit to lure birds, pass undigested through their intestinal tracts and be voided miles away.

The ramifications of this biological invention were endless. Plants traveled as they had never traveled before. They got into strange environments heretofore never entered by the old spore plants or stiff pine-cone-seed plants. The well-fed, carefully cherished little embryos raised their heads everywhere. Many of the older plants with more primitive reproductive mechanisms began to fade away under this unequal contest. They contracted their range into secluded environments. Some, like the giant redwoods, lingered on as relics; many vanished entirely.

The world of the giants was a dying world. These fantastic little seeds skipping and hopping and flying about the woods and valleys brought with them an amazing adaptability. If our whole lives had not been spent in the midst of it, it would astound us. The old, stiff, sky-reaching wooden world had changed into something that glowed here and there with strange colors, put out queer, unheard-of fruits and little intricately carved seed cases, and, most important of all, produced concentrated foods in a way that the land had never seen before, or dreamed of back in the fish-eating, leaf-crunching days of the dinosaurs.

That food came from three sources, all produced by the reproductive system of the flowering plants. There were the tantalizing nectars and pollen intended to draw insects for pollenizing purposes, and which are responsible also for that wonderful jeweled creation, the hummingbird. There were the juicy and enticing fruits to attract larger animals, and in which tough-coated seeds were concealed, as in the tomato, for example. Then, as if this were not enough, there was the food in the actual seed itself, the food intended to nourish the embryo. All over the world, like hot corn in a popper, these incredible elaborations of the flowering plants kept exploding. In a movement that was almost instantaneous, geologically speaking, the angiosperms had taken over the world. Grass was beginning to cover the bare earth until, today, there are over six thousand species. All kinds of vines and bushes squirmed and writhed under new trees with flying seeds.

The explosion was having its effect on animal life also. Specialized groups of insects were arising to feed on the new sources of food and, incidentally and unknowingly, to pollinate the plant. The flowers bloomed and bloomed in ever larger and more spectacular varieties. Some were pale unearthly night flowers intended to lure moths in the evening twilight, some among the orchids even took the shape of female spiders in order to attract wandering males, some flamed redly in the light of noon or twinkled modestly in the meadow grasses. Intricate mechanisms splashed pollen on the breasts of hummingbirds, or stamped it on the bellies of black, grumbling bees droning assiduously from blossom to blossom. Honey ran, insects multiplied, and even the descendants of that toothed and ancient lizard-bird had become strangely altered. Equipped with prodding beaks instead of biting teeth they pecked the seeds and gobbled the insects that were really converted nectar.

Across the planet grasslands were now spreading. A slow continental upthrust which had been a part of the early Age of Flowers had cooled the world's climates. The stalking reptiles and the leather-winged black imps of the seashore cliffs had vanished. Only birds roamed the air now, hot-blooded and high-speed metabolic machines.

The mammals, too, had survived and were venturing into new domains, staring about perhaps a bit bewildered at their sudden eminence now that the thunder lizards were gone. Many of them, beginning as small browsers upon leaves in the forest, began to venture out upon this new sunlit world of the grass. Grass has a high silica content and demands a new type of very tough and resistant tooth enamel, but the seeds taken incidentally in the cropping of the grass are highly nutritious. A new world had opened out for the warm-blooded mammals. Great herbivores like the mammoths, horses and bisons appeared. Skulking about them had arisen savage flesh-feeding carnivores like the now extinct dire wolves and the saber-toothed tiger.

Flesh eaters though these creatures were, they were

being sustained on nutritious grasses one step removed. Their fierce energy was being maintained on a high, effective level, through hot days and frosty nights, by the concentrated energy of the angiosperms. That energy, thirty per cent or more of the weight of the entire plant among some of the cereal grasses, was being accumulated and concentrated in the rich proteins and fats of the enormous game herds of the grasslands.

On the edge of the forest, a strange, old-fashioned animal still hesitated. His body was the body of a tree dweller, and though tough and knotty by human standards, he was, in terms of that world into which he gazed, a weakling. His teeth, though strong for chewing on the tough fruits of the forest, or for crunching an occasional unwary bird caught with his prehensile hands, were not the tearing sabers of the great cats. He had a passion for lifting himself up to see about, in his restless, roving curiosity. He would run a little stiffly and uncertainly, perhaps, on his hind legs, but only in those rare moments when he ventured out upon the ground. All this was the legacy of his climbing days; he had a hand with flexible fingers and no fine specialized hoofs upon which to gallop like the wind.

If he had any idea of competing in that new world, he had better forget it; teeth or hooves, he was much too late for either. He was a ne'-er-do-well, an in-betweener. Nature had not done well by him. It was as if she had hesitated and never quite made up her mind. Perhaps as a consequence he had a malicious gleam in his eye, the gleam of an outcast who has been left nothing and knows he is going to have to take what he gets. One day a little band of these odd apes — for apes they were — shambled out upon the grass; the human story had begun.

Apes were to become men, in the inscrutable wisdom of nature, because flowers had produced seeds and fruits in such tremendous quantities that a new and totally different store of energy had become available in concentrated form. Impressive as the slow-moving, dim-brained dinosaurs had been, it is doubtful if their age had supported anything like the diversity of life that now rioted across the planet or flashed in and out among the trees. Down on the grass by a streamside, one of those apes with inquisitive fingers turned over a stone and hefted it vaguely. The group clucked together in a throaty tongue and moved off through the tall grass foraging for seeds and insects. The one still held, sniffed, and hefted the stone he had found. He liked the feel of it in his fingers. The attack on the animal world was about to begin.

If one could run the story of that first human group like a speeded-up motion picture through a million years of time, one might see the stone in the hand change to the flint ax and the torch. All that swarming grassland world with its giant bison and trumpeting mammoths would go down in ruin to feed the insatiable and growing numbers of a carnivore who, like the great cats before him, was taking his energy indirectly from the grass. Later he found fire and it altered the tough meats and drained their energy even faster into a stomach ill adapted for the ferocious turn man's habits had taken.

His limbs grew longer, he strode more purposefully over the grass. The stolen energy that would take man across the continents would fail him at last. The great Ice Age herds were destined to vanish. When they did so, another hand like the hand that grasped the stone by the river long ago would pluck a handful of grass seed and hold it contemplatively.

In that moment, the golden towers of man, his swarming millions, his turning wheels, the vast learning of his packed libraries, would glimmer dimly there in the ancestor of wheat, a few seeds held in a muddy hand. Without the gift of flowers and the infinite diversity of their fruits, man and bird, if they had continued to exist at all, would be today unrecognizable. Archaeopteryx, the lizard-bird, might still be snapping at beetles on a sequoia limb; man might still be a nocturnal insectivore gnawing a roach in the dark. The weight of a petal has changed the face of the world and made it ours.

Aldo
Leopold

"ESCUDILLA"

Life in Arizona was bounded underfoot by grama
grass, overhead by sky, and on the horizon by
Escudilla.

To the north of the mountain you rode on honey-
colored plains. Look up anywhere, any time, and you
saw Escudilla.

To the east you rode over a confusion of wooded
mesas. Each hollow seemed its own small world,
soaked in sun, fragrant with juniper, and cozy with
the chatter of piñon jays. But top out on a ridge and
you at once became a speck in an immensity. On its
edge hung Escudilla.

To the south lay the tangled canyons of Blue River,
full of whitetails, wild turkeys, and wilder cattle.
When you missed a saucy buck waving his goodbye
over the skyline, and looked down your sights to
wonder why, you looked at a far blue mountain:
Escudilla . . .

There was, in fact, only one place from which you did not see Escudilla on the skyline: that was the top of Escudilla itself. Up there you could not see the mountain, but you could feel it. The reason was the big bear.

Old Bigfoot was a robber-baron, and Escudilla was his castle. Each spring, when the warm winds had softened the shadows on the snow, the old grizzly crawled out of his hibernation den in the rock slides and, descending the mountain, bashed in the head of a cow. Eating his fill, he climbed back to his crags, and there summered peaceably on marmots, conies, berries, and roots.

I once saw one of his kills. The cow's skull and neck were pulp, as if she had collided head-on with a fast freight.

No one ever saw the old bear, but in the muddy springs about the base of the cliffs you saw his incredible tracks. Seeing them made the most hard-bitten cowboys aware of bear. Wherever they rode they saw the mountain, and when they saw the mountain they thought of bear. Campfire conversation ran to beef, *bailes* and bear. Bigfoot claimed for his own only a cow a year, and a few square miles of useless rocks, but his personality pervaded the county.

Those were the days when progress first came to the cow county. Progress had various emissaries.

One was the first transcontinental automobilist. The cowboys understood this breaker of roads; he talked the same breezy bravado as any breaker of broncos . . .

They marveled, too, at the telephone engineer who strung wires on the junipers and brought instantaneous messages from town. An old man asked whether the wire could bring him a side of bacon.

One spring, progress sent still another emissary, a government trapper, a sort of St. George in overalls, seeking dragons to slay at government expense. Were there, he asked, any destructive animals in need of slaying? Yes, there was the big bear.

The trapper packed his mule and headed for Escudilla.

In a month he was back, his mule staggering under a heavy hide. There was only one barn in town big enough to dry it on. He had tried traps, poison, and all his usual wiles to no avail. Then he had erected a set-gun in a defile through which only the bear could pass, and waited. The last grizzly walked into the string and shot himself.

It was June. The pelt was foul, patchy, and worthless. It seemed to us rather an insult to deny the last grizzly the chance to leave a good pelt as a memorial to his race. All he left was a skull in the National Museum, and a quarrel among scientists over the Latin name of the skull.

It was only after we pondered on these things that we began to wonder who wrote the rules for progress.

Since the beginning, time had gnawed at the basaltic hulk of Escudilla, wasting, waiting, and building. Time built three things on the old mountain, a venerable aspect, a community of minor animals and plants, and a grizzly.

The government trapper who took the grizzly knew

he had made Escudilla safe for cows. He did not know he had toppled the spire off an edifice a-building since the morning stars sang together.

The bureau chief who sent the trapper was a biologist versed in the architecture of evolution, but he did not know that spires might be as important as cows. He did not foresee that within two decades the cow country would become tourist country, and as such have greater need of bears than of beefsteaks.

The Congressmen who voted money to clear the ranges of bears were the sons of pioneers. They acclaimed the superior virtues of the frontiersman, but they strove with might and main to make an end of the frontier.

We forest officers, who acquiesced in the extinguishment of the bear, knew a local rancher who had plowed up a dagger engraved with the name of one of Coronado's captains. We spoke harshly of the Spaniards who, in their zeal for gold and converts, had needlessly extinguished the native Indians. It did not occur to us that we, too, were the captains of an invasion too sure of its own righteousness.

Escudilla still hangs on the horizon, but when you see it you no longer think of bear. It's only a mountain now.

Robert
Pirsig

ZEN AND THE ART OF
MOTORCYCLE MAINTENANCE

Mountains should be climbed with as little effort as possible and without desire. The reality of your own nature should determine the speed. If you become restless, speed up. If you become winded, slow down. You climb the mountain in an equilibrium between restlessness and exhaustion. Then, when you're no longer thinking ahead, each footstep isn't just a means to an end but a unique event in itself. *This* leaf has jagged edges. *This* rock looks loose. From *this* place the snow is less visible, even though closer. These are things you should notice anyway. To live only for some future goal is shallow. It's the sides of the mountains which sustain life, not the top . . .

Anatole France

Do not try to satisfy your vanity by teaching a great many things. Awaken people's curiosity. It is enough to open minds; do not overload them. Put there just a spark. If there is some good inflammable stuff, it will catch fire.

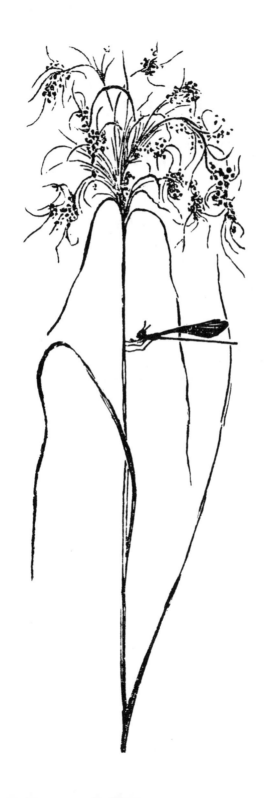

Henry David Thoreau

The birds I heard today, which, fortunately, did not come within the scope of my science, sang as freshly as if it had been the first morning of creation.

Sally Carrighar

HOME TO THE WILDERNESS

I held a blue flower in my hand, probably a wild aster, wondering what its name was, and then thought that human names for natural things are superfluous. Nature herself does not name them. The important thing is to *know* this flower, look at its color until the blueness becomes as real as a keynote of music. Look at the exquisite yellow flowerettes in the center, become very small with them. *Be* the flower, be the trees, the blowing grasses. Fly with the birds, jump with the squirrel!

John
Moffitt

"TO LOOK AT ANY THING"

To look at any thing,
  If you would know that thing,
You must look at it long:
To look at this green and say
'I have seen spring in these
woods,' will not do — you must
Be the thing you see:
You must be the dark snakes of
Stems and ferny plumes of leaves,
You must enter in
To the small silences between
The leaves,
You must take your time
And touch the very peace
They issue from.

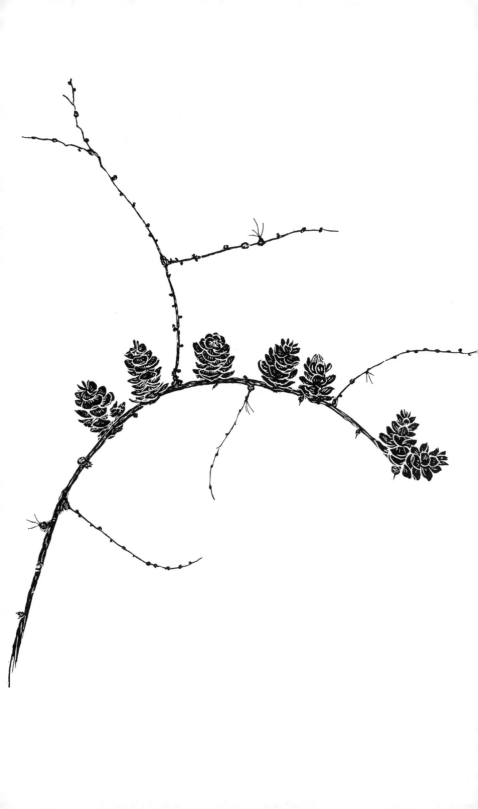

Gary
Snyder

"PINE TREE TOPS"

In the blue night
frost haze, the sky glows
with the moon
pine tree tops
bend snow-blue, fade
into sky, frost, starlight.
the creak of boots.
rabbit tracks, deer tracks,
what do we know.

Chief Seattle

You must teach your children that the ground beneath their feet is the ashes of our grandfathers. So that they will respect the land, tell your children that the earth is rich with the lives of our kin. Teach your children what we have taught our children — that the earth is our mother. Whatever befalls the earth, befalls the sons of the earth. If men spit upon the ground, they spit upon themselves.

This we know. The earth does not belong to man; man belongs to the earth. This we know. All things are connected like the blood which unites one family. All things are connected.

Whatever befalls the earth befalls the sons of the earth. Man did not weave the web of life; he is merely a strand in it. Whatever he does to the web, he does to himself . . .

EARTH SPIRIT

EARTH SPIRIT

STEVE VAN MATRE

THIS SECTION IS ABOUT GIVING UP OLD WAYS OF
SEEING, about loving the earth as a whole, about tapping
into the universal flow of life, and about simplifying, yet
dreaming. But most of all, it is about our needs as an
unusual species of life, needs that must be met if we are to
respond to the earth's cries for help.

First, we need a new kind of love to temper our
passions. Like the chief suggests in the story of jumping
mouse in this section, we must give up our childish ways
of seeing things. Our love has been egocentric, it must
become ecocentric. For many of us, our approach to
love has been like loving a toe, an earlobe, or an elbow.
It's been an unhealthy captivation with the parts rather
than the whole. We must learn to love ourselves less and
the earth more. This will not be an easy task for we live
in the age of nonsense. Bombarded with thousands of
messages each day that proclaim how to be loved
instead of how to be loving, we have learned to love
objects instead of processes. We need to broaden our

scope, to change our frame of reference. We shouldn't feel sorry for jumping mouse. He lived life fully. His love for security did not restrict his vision of the world. His love for the comforts of life did not blind him to its realities. His love led him to discover a larger family of life, and he gave of himself so that others might live. Jumping mouse gained control of his fears and his love blossomed.

Second, we need new rituals and parables to remind us of our earthbound roles. A man in India explained to this writer that his mother taught him as a child to pat the earth each morning when he awoke, apologizing for the need of walking upon it. This is the kind of reminder we need today, a way of focusing our attention on what is truly important here. In the Hindu parable of Indra's net, the primeval god Indra casts his net of life into the voids of space. At the junction of every pair of threads in his net of life there is a crystal bead, and each crystal bead is a living thing, shining forth with its own glow, its own radiance into space. And the glow of every crystal bead in the net of life reflects the glow of every other bead.

This is the way life works on earth. Each living thing is a spark of sunlight energy, a crystal bead in the net of life. As humans, like other forms of life, we are only here for a few moments, a mere glistening in time on the film of life covering the planet. When we die, the sunlight energy holding the building materials together flickers out, and those materials that make us up are eventually taken up through the threads of the net by other living things to be used again. Life on the earth represents a continual process of birth and death, decay and rebirth as the building materials are used over and over again by all living things. You see, the earth is not like our mother, it is our first mother. The sky is not like our father, it is our first father. The union of earth and sky beget all living things in this oasis in space.

Third, we need to reach out and embrace life anew. Yes, to hug a tree, to play with the wind, to wear a new costume, to whisper secrets to a flower, to seek beauty in life's becomings. We must not be afraid to act joyously, to display our curiosity, to seek adventure. When asked how he remained so youthful at age 72, Ashley Montagu replied, *"The trick is to die young as late as possible."* In this context, we should all strive to die so young.

According to the story of the origins of Zen, the founder of Buddhism had been asked to present a talk on truth to his followers. However, instead of talking, he merely took a flower from a nearby vase and held it up, gazing at it. Everyone in the group was puzzled by this unusual behavior, but suddenly one of them smiled knowingly. This disciple became the first teacher of Zen. In a sudden flash he had recognized the point the Buddha was making. Words are just that, words, and nothing more. Reality lies in doing, not thinking.

We have become so full of our own importance that we can no longer see much of our roleplaying and posturing and verbalizing for what they are, as Alan Watts suggests, merely the attention-getting antics of a different species. To get out of our own light, our own static a bit, we must take unusual steps, perhaps something as simple as going out at night without a light as Wendell Berry recommends here, or something as complicated as Thoreau's retreat to Walden Pond.

Fourth, we need new watchmen to call our attention to the dangers ahead. On ships at sea men stood watch throughout the night, prepared to alert the passengers to unseen dangers. As we sail the cosmic seas our life vessel may have entered its darkest hours, but the dangers here are all on board. We need a new generation to sound the alarm, a new crew of men and women to help set the course for a safe passage. There is no doubt that turbulent days lie ahead. Will we eventually become a death ship, an eternal reminder in the universe of the dangers inherent in the development of higher forms of life? Or as someone else has expressed it, will our epitaph read: "'Next time,' God said, 'no brains.'"

Fifth, we need new visions toward which to dedicate our lives. After all, ideas and their symbols change the world. There is an Arabian tale about a prince who inherited a city, only to find his inheritance in chaos. The traders from the caravans had preyed upon the townspeople and, instead of resisting, the townspeople had fallen victim to the evils of corruption and thievery. In an effort to change the situation the prince heeded the urgings of his ministers and proclaimed a new and tougher code of laws. However, instead of getting better, things got worse. The disputes, the robberies, the violence increased, and in the end, the caravans began bypassing the impoverished city altogether. At last, in desperation the prince commanded that the best craftsmen of the kingdom should be brought to him. When they had gathered, the prince directed them to build, in great secrecy, a model that he had designed of the most perfect city imaginable. When the artisans had completed their task, the prince had the model installed behind a special screen in the main mosque. Next, he ordered that all newcomers arriving at the city gates should be taken to see the model city, but instructed to tell no one of what they had seen, and no one else was to be allowed behind the screen.

The newcomers, overwhelmed by their vision of an incredibly beautiful city, left the mosque radiant from the experience. The townspeople asked the newcomers over and over what they had seen, but to no avail. Day after day the appearance of the newcomers continued to arouse the townspeople's curiosity, until at last, they went to the palace and demanded to see what was hidden behind the screen in the mosque. The prince agreed; the people were also transformed by the experience, and the prince's dream of a model city became a reality.

Paraphrasing George Bernard Shaw, Robert Kennedy said, "*Some men see things as they are and say why. I dream things that never were and say why not.*" Let's dream new dreams together. Why not a world of millions instead of billions of human passengers? Why not a world where the threat of nuclear annihilation is only a vague, unpleasant memory? Why not a world of small towns spaced miles apart? Why not a world where all of us, not just some of us, pursue more physical, labor-intensive lifestyles closer to the land? Why not a world where there are more tigers in the wild than in zoos?

Let's cage ourselves and let the animals run free.
Let's tear down our egocentric structures and systems and build anew.
Let's find new stars and new songs to follow.
And finally, as Thoreau suggests, let's build some foundations under our dreams.
For if we have the prowess to destroy the earth, then we can surely save it.

Solomon Ibn-Gabirol

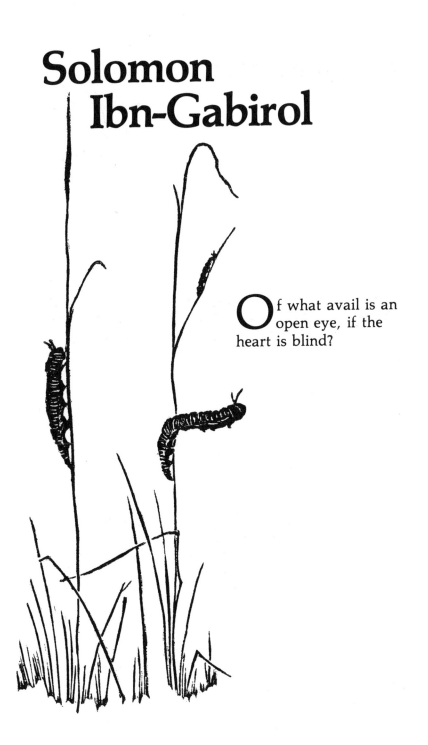

Of what avail is an open eye, if the heart is blind?

Crowfoot

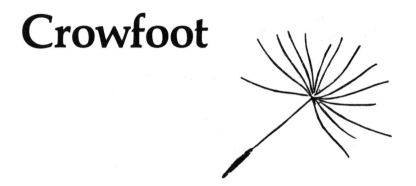

What is life? It is the flash of a firefly in the night. It is the breath of a buffalo in the winter time. It is the little shadow which runs across the grass and loses itself in the Sunset.

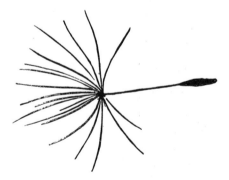

Albert Schweitzer

"REVERENCE FOR LIFE"

L et a man once begin to think about the mystery of
his life and the links which connect him with the
life that fills the world, and he cannot but bring to
bear upon his own life and all other life that comes
within his reach the principle of reverence for life . . .

Gary Snyder

"PRAYER FOR THE GREAT FAMILY"

G ratitude to Mother Earth , sailing through night and day –
and to her soil: rich, rare, and sweet
in our minds so be it.

Gratitude to Plants, the sun-facing light-changing leaf
and fine root-hairs; standing still through wind
and rain; their dance is in the flowing spiral grain
in our minds so be it.

Gratitude to Air, bearing the soaring Swift and the silent
Owl at dawn. Breath of our song
clear spirit breeze
in our minds so be it.

Gratitude to Wild Beings, our brothers, teaching secrets,
freedoms, and ways; who share with us their milk;
self-complete, brave and aware
in our minds so be it.

Gratitude to Water: clouds, lakes, rivers, glaciers;
　　holding or releasing; streaming through all
　　our bodies salty seas
　　　　in our minds so be it.

Gratitude to the Sun: blinding pulsing light through
　　trunks of trees, through mists, warming caves where
　　bears and snakes sleep — he who wakes us —
　　　　in our minds so be it.

Gratitude to the Great Sky
　　who holds billions of stars — and goes yet beyond that —
　　beyond all powers, and thoughts
　　and yet is within us —
　　Grandfather Space.
　　The Mind is his Wife.

　　　　so be it.

　　(after a Mohawk prayer)

Robinson Jeffers

"THE ANSWER"

The greatest beauty
is organic wholeness,
the wholeness of life and things,
the divine beauty of the universe.
Love that, not man apart from that . . .

Chief Luther Standing Bear

LAND OF THE SPOTTED EAGLE

The old people came literally to love the soil and they sat or reclined on the ground with a feeling of being close to a mothering power. It was good for the skin to touch the earth and the old people liked to remove their moccasins and walk with bare feet on the sacred earth. Their tipis were built upon the earth and their altars were made of earth. The birds that flew into the air came to rest upon the earth and it was the final abiding place of all things that lived and grew. The soil was soothing, strengthening, cleansing and healing.

John
Neihardt

BLACK ELK SPEAKS

You have noticed that everything an Indian does is in a circle, and that is because the Power of the World always works in circles, and everything tries to be round. In the old days when we were a strong and happy people, all our power came to us from the sacred hoop of the nation and so long as the hoop was unbroken the people flourished. The flowering tree was the living center of the hoop, and the circle of the four quarters nourished it. The east gave peace and light, the south gave warmth, the west gave rain, and the north with its cold and mighty wind gave strength and endurance. This knowledge came to us from the outer world with our religion. Everything the Power of the World does is in a circle. The Sky is round and I have heard that the earth is round like a ball and so are all the stars. The Wind, in its greatest power, whirls. Birds make their nests in circles ... The sun comes forth and goes down again in a circle. The moon does the same, and both are round.

Even the seasons form a great circle in their changing, and always come back again to where they were. The life of a man is a circle from childhood to childhood and so it is in everything where power moves. Our tipis were round like the nests of birds and these were always set in a circle, the nation's hoop, a nest of many nests where the Great Spirit meant for us to hatch our children.

Frank Waters

THE MAN WHO KILLED THE DEER

They stood in a somber circle about a lofty pine in the forest. Their faces were respectful and their dark eyes shone with wonder, but the blades in their hands gleamed bright and sharp. There were many of them, and it was Palemon who made the prayer-talk before they cut their brother down.

"We know your life is as precious as ours. We know that we all are children of the same Mother Earth, of Our Father Sun. But we also know that one life must sometimes give way to another, so that the one great life of all may continue unbroken. So we ask your permission, we obtain your consent to this killing."

So they cut him down, he in their midst who had stood there tall and sound and proud before they were yet grown. And it was well with them and with him who had spiritually assented to their ritualistic request for his sacrifice.

Herbert Spinden

"SONG OF THE SKY LOOM"

Oh our Mother the Earth,
 oh our Father the Sky ...
weave for us a garment
        of brightness;

May the warp be the
        white light of morning,
May the weft be the
        red light of evening,
May the fringes be
        the falling rain,
May the border be
        the standing rainbow ...

That we may walk fittingly where
        birds sing ...
        where grass is green,

Oh our Mother the Earth,
        oh our Father the sky!

Sigurd Olson

REFLECTIONS FROM THE NORTH COUNTRY

Beauty is composed of many things and never stands alone. It is part of horizons, blue in the distance, great primeval silences, knowledge of all things of the earth ... It is so fragile it can be destroyed by a sound or thought. It may be infinitesimally small or encompass the universe itself. It comes in a swift conception wherever nature has not been disturbed.

LISTENING POINT

I must leave it as beautiful as I found it. Nothing must ever happen there that might detract in the slightest from what it now had. I would enjoy it and discover all that was to be found there and learn as time went on that here perhaps was all I might ever hope to know.

As I sat there on the rock I realized that, in spite of the closeness of civilization and the changes that hemmed it in, this remnant of the old wilderness would speak to me of silence and solitude, of belonging and wonder and beauty. Though the point was only a small part of the vastness reaching far to the arctic, from it I could survey the whole. While it would be mine for only a short time, this glaciated shore with its twisted trees and caribou moss would grow into my life and into the lives of all who shared it with me.

I named this place Listening Point because only when one comes to listen, only when one is aware and still, can things be seen and heard. Everyone has a listening-point somewhere. It does not have to be in the north or close to the wilderness, but some place of quiet where the universe can be contemplated with awe.

John
Burroughs

BIRDS AND POETS

The beauty of nature includes all that is called beautiful, as its flower; and all that is not called beautiful, as its stalk and roots. Indeed, when I go to the woods or the fields, or ascend to the hilltop, I do not seem to be gazing upon beauty at all, but to be breathing it like the air. I am not dazzled or astonished; I am in no hurry to look lest it be gone. I would not have the litter and debris removed, or the banks trimmed, or the ground painted. What I enjoy is commensurate with the earth and sky itself. It clings to the rocks and trees; it is kindred to the roughness and savagery; it rises from every tangle and chasm; it perches on the dry oak-stubs with the hawks and buzzards; the crows shed it from their wings and weave it into their nests of coarse sticks; the fox barks it, the cattle low it, and every mountain path leads to its haunts. I am not a spectator of, but a participator in it. It is not an adornment; its roots strike to the centre of the earth.

Alan W. Watts

NATURE, MAN AND WOMAN

Perhaps we may now begin to see why men have an almost universal tendency to seek relief from their own kind among the trees and plants, the mountains and waters. There is an easy and rather cheap sophistication in mocking the love of nature, but there is always something profound and essential in the universal theme of poetry, however hackneyed. For hundreds of years the great poets of East and West have given expression to this basically human love of "communing with nature," a phrase which in present-day intellectual circles seems to have acquired a slightly ridiculous tone. Presumably it is regarded as one of those "escapes from reality" so much condemned by those who restrict reality to what one reads about in the newspapers.

But perhaps the reason for this love of nonhuman nature is that communion with it restores to us a level of our own human nature at which we are still sane, free from humbug, and untouched by anxieties about the meaning and purpose of our lives. For what we call "nature" is free from a certain kind of scheming and self-importance. The birds and beasts indeed pursue their business of eating and breeding with the utmost devotion. But they do not justify it; they do not pretend that it serves higher ends, or that it makes a significant contribution to the progress of the world.

This is not meant to sound unkind to human beings, because the point is not so simple as that the birds are right and we are wrong. The point is that rapport with the marvelously purposeless world of nature gives us new eyes for ourselves — eyes in which our very self-importance is not condemned, but seen as something quite other than what it imagines itself to be. In this light all the weirdly abstract and pompous pursuits of men are suddenly transformed into natural marvels of the same order as the immense beaks of the toucans and hornbills, the fabulous tails of the birds of paradise, the towering necks of the giraffes, and the vividly polychromed posteriors of the baboons. Seen thus, neither as something to be condemned nor in its accustomed aspect of serious worth, the self-importance of man dissolves in laughter. His insistent purposefulness and his extraordinary preoccupation with abstractions are, while perfectly natural, overdone — like the vast bodies of the dinosaurs. As means of survival and adaptation they have been overplayed, producing a species too cunning and too practical for its own good, and which for this very reason stands in need of the "dead cat's head" philosophy. For this is the philosophy which, like nature, has no purpose or consequence other than itself.

Lao
Tzu

TAO TE CHING

Those who know do not talk.
Those who talk do not know.

Keep your mouth closed.
Guard your senses.
Temper your sharpness.
Simplify your problems.
Mask your brightness.
Be at one with the dust of the earth.
This is primal union.

He who has achieved this state
Is unconcerned with friends and enemies,
With good and harm, with honor and disgrace.
This therefore is the highest state of man.

Seng-ts'an

"HSIN-HSIN MING"

The wise person does not strive;
The ignorant man ties himself up . . .
If you work on your mind
        with your mind,
How can you avoid an
        immense confusion?

Henry David Thoreau

WALDEN

Why should we be in such desperate haste to succeed and in such desperate enterprises? If a man does not keep pace with his companions, perhaps it is because he hears a different drummer. Let him step to the music which he hears, however measured or far away. It is not important that he should mature as soon as an apple tree or an oak. Shall he turn his spring into summer? If the condition of things which we were made for is not yet, what were any reality which we can substitute? We will not be shipwrecked on a vain reality. Shall we with pains erect a heaven of blue glass over ourselves, though when it is done we shall be sure to gaze still at the true ethereal heaven far above, as if the former were not?

The greater part of what my neighbors call good, I believe in my soul to be bad, and if I repent of anything, it is very likely to be my good behavior. What demon possessed me that I behaved so well? You may say the wisest thing you can, old man — you who have lived seventy years, not without honor of a kind — I hear an irresistible voice which invites me away from all that. One generation abandons the enterprises of another like stranded vessels.

I went to the woods because I wished to live deliberately, to front only the essential facts of life, and see if I could not learn what it had to teach, and not, when I came to die, discover that I had not lived. I did not wish to live what was not life, living is so dear; nor did I wish to practice resignation, unless it was quite necessary. I wanted to live deep and suck out all the marrow of life, to live so sturdily and Spartan-like as to put to rout all that was not life, to cut a broad swath and shave close, to drive life into a corner, and reduce it to its lowest terms, and, if it proved to be mean, why then to get the whole and genuine meanness of it, and publish its meanness to the world; or if it were sublime, to know it by experience, and be able to give a true account of it in my next excursion. For most men, it appears to me, are in a strange uncertainty about it, whether it is of the devil or of God, and have somewhat hastily concluded that it is the chief end of man here to "glorify God and enjoy Him forever."

Let us spend one day as deliberately as Nature, and not be thrown off the track by every nutshell and mosquito's wing that falls on the rails. Let us rise early and fast, or break fast, gently and without perturbation; let company come and let company go, let the bells ring and the children cry — determined to make a day of it. Why should we knock under and go with the stream? Let us not be upset and overwhelmed in that terrible rapid and whirlpool called a dinner, situated in the meridian shallows. Weather this danger and you are safe, for the rest of the way is down hill. With unrelaxed nerves, with morning vigor, sail by it, looking another way, tied to the mast like Ulysses. If the engine whistles, let it whistle till it is hoarse for its pains. If the bell rings, why should we run? We will consider what kind of music they are like. Let us settle ourselves, and work and wedge our feet downward through the mud and slush of opinion, and prejudice, and tradition, and delusion, and appearance, that alluvion which covers the globe, through Paris and London, through New York and Boston and Concord, through Church and State, through poetry and philosophy and religion, till we come to a hard bottom and rocks in place, which we can call *reality*, and say, This is, and not mistake; and then begin, having a *point d'appui*, below freshet and frost and fire, a place where you might found a wall or a state, or set a lamp-post safely, or perhaps a gauge, not a Nilometer, but a Realometer, that future ages might know how deep a freshet of shams and appearances had gathered from time to time. If you stand right fronting and face to face to a fact, you will see the sun glimmer on both its surfaces, as if it were a cimeter, and feel its sweet edge dividing you through the heart and marrow, and so you will happily conclude your mortal career. Be it life or death, we crave only reality. If we are really dying, let us hear the rattle in our throats and feel cold in the extremities; if we are alive, let us go about our business.

Time is but the stream I go a-fishing in. I drink at it; but while I drink I see the sandy bottom and detect how shallow it is. Its thin current slides away, but eternity remains. I would drink deeper; fish in the sky, whose bottom is pebbly with stars. I cannot count one. I know not the first letter of the alphabet. I have always been regretting that I was not as wise as the day I was born. The intellect is a cleaver; it discerns and rifts its way into the secret of things. I do not wish to be any more busy with my hands than is necessary. My head is hands and feet. I feel all my best faculties concentrated in it. My instinct tells me that my head is an organ for burrowing, as some creatures use their snout and forepaws, and with it I would mine and burrow my way through these hills. I think that the richest vein is somewhere hereabouts; so by the divining-rod and thin rising vapors I judge; and here I will begin to mine.

I did not read books the first summer; I hoed beans. Nay, I often did better than this. There were times when I could not afford to sacrifice the bloom of the present moment to any work, whether of the head or hands. I love a broad margin to my life. Sometimes, in a summer morning, having taken my accustomed bath, I sat in my sunny doorway from sunrise till noon, rapt in a reverie, amidst the pines and hickories and sumachs, in undisturbed solitude and stillness, while the birds sang around or flitted noiselessly through the house, until by the sun falling in at my west window, or the noise of some traveller's wagon on the distant highway, I was reminded of the lapse of time. I grew in those seasons like corn in the night, and they were far better than any work of the hands would have been. They were not time subtracted from my life, but so much over and above my usual allowance. I realized what the Orientals mean by contemplation and the forsaking of works. For the most part, I minded not how the hours went. The day advanced as if to light some work of mine; it was morning, and lo, now it is evening, and nothing memorable is accomplished. Instead of singing like the birds, I silently smiled at my incessant good fortune. As the sparrow had its trill, sitting on the hickory before my door, so had I my chuckle or suppressed warble which he might hear out of my nest. My days were not days of the week, bearing the stamp of any heathen deity, nor were they minced into hours and fretted by the ticking of a clock; for I lived like the Puri Indians, of whom it is said that "for yesterday, today, and tomorrow they have only one word, and they express the variety of meaning by pointing backward for yesterday, forward for tomorrow, and overhead for the passing day." This was sheer idleness to my fellow-townsmen, no doubt; but if the birds and flowers had tried me by their standard, I should not have been found wanting. A man must find his occasions in himself, it is true. The natural day is very calm, and will hardly reprove his indolence.

I left the woods for as good a reason as I went there. Perhaps it seemed to me that I had several more lives to live, and could not spare any more time for that one. It is remarkable how easily and insensibly we fall into a particular route, and make a beaten track for ourselves. I had not lived there a week before my feet wore a path from my door to the pond-side; and though it is five or six years since I trod it, it is still quite distinct. It is true, I fear, that others may have fallen into it, and so helped to keep it open. The surface of the earth is soft and impressible by the feet of men; and so with the paths which the mind travels. How worn and dusty, then, must be the highways of the world, how deep the ruts of tradition and conformity! I did not wish to take a cabin passage, but rather to go before the mast and on the deck of the world, for there I could best see the moonlight amid the mountains. I do not wish to go below now.

I learned this, at least, by my experiment; that if one advances confidently in the direction of his dreams, and endeavors to live the life which he has imagined, he will meet with a success unexpected in common hours. He will put some things behind, will pass an invisible boundary; new, universal, and more liberal laws will begin to establish themselves around and within him; or the old laws be expanded, and interpreted in his favor in a more liberal sense and he will live with the license of a higher order of beings. In proportion as he simplifies his life, the laws of the universe will appear less complex, and solitude will not be solitude, nor poverty poverty, nor weakness weakness. If you have built castles in the air, your work need not be lost; that is where they should be. Now put the foundations under them.

Antoine de Saint Exupéry

THE LITTLE PRINCE

"All men have the stars," he answered, "but they are not the same things for different people. For some, who are travelers, the stars are guides. For others they are no more than little lights in the sky. For others, who are scholars, they are problems. For my businessman they were wealth ... You — you alone — have the stars as no one else has them ..."

"I wonder whether the stars are set alight in heaven so that one day each one of us may find his own again...."

"...the stars, the desert — what gives them their beauty is something that is invisible!"

"And now here is my secret, a very simple secret: It is only with the heart that one can see rightly; what is essential is invisible to the eye."

Wendell Berry

"TO KNOW THE DARK"

To go in the dark with a light is to know the light.
To know the dark, go dark. Go without sight,
and find that the dark, too, blooms and sings,
and is traveled by dark feet and dark wings.

Winston
Abbott

"HAVE YOU HEARD THE CRICKET SONG?"

t wilight is a time for sharing — and a time for
 remembering — sharing the fragrance of the
cooling earth — the shadows of the gathering
dusk —

　　　here our two worlds meet and pass — the
frantic sounds of man grow dimmer as the light
recedes — the unhurried rhythm of the other
world swells in volume as the darkness
deepens —

　　　　　it is not strange that discord has
no place in this great symphony of sound —
　　　　　it is not strange that a sense
of peace descends upon all living things —
　　　　　it is not strange that
memories burn more brightly — as the things of
substance lose their line and form in the softness
of the dark —

twilight is a time for sharing — and a
time for remembering — remembering the things of
beauty wasted by our careless hands — our frequent
disregard of other living things — the many songs
unheard because we would not listen —

listen tonight with all the
wisdom of your spirit — listen too with
all the compassion of your heart —
lest there come another night —
when there is only silence —

a great
and
total
silence —

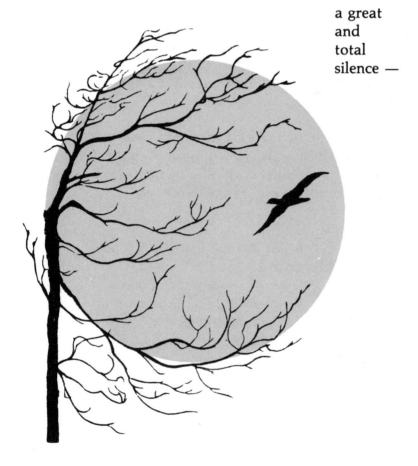

Thomas Merton

"RAIN AND THE RHINOCEROS"

What a thing it is to sit absolutely alone,
in the forest, at night, cherished by this
wonderful, unintelligible,
perfectly innocent speech,
the most comforting speech in the world,
the talk that rain makes by itself all over the ridges,
and the talk of the watercourses everywhere in the
hollows!
   Nobody started it, nobody is going to stop it.
It will talk as long as it wants, this rain.
As long as it talks I am going to listen.

Annie Dillard

PILGRIM AT TINKER CREEK

I t is sheer coincidence that my hunk of the creek is strewn with boulders. I never merited this grace, that when I face upstream I scent the virgin breath of mountains, I feel a spray of mist on my cheeks and lips, I hear a ceaseless splash and susurrus, a sound of water not merely poured smoothly down air to fill a steady pool, but tumbling live about, over, under, around, between, through an intricate speckling of rock. It is sheer coincidence that upstream from me the creek's bed is ridged in horizontal croppings of sandstone. I never merited this grace, that when I face upstream I see the light on the water careening towards me, inevitably, freely, down a graded series of terraces like the balanced winged platforms on an infinite, inexhaustible font. "Ho, if you are thirsty, come down to the water; ho, if you are hungry, come and sit and eat." This is the present, at last. I can pat the puppy any time I want. This is the now, this flickering, broken light, this air that the wind of the

future presses down my throat, pumping me buoyant and giddy with praise.

My God, I look at the creek. It is the answer to Merton's prayer, "Give us time!" It never stops. If I seek the senses and skill of children, the information of a thousand books, the innocence of puppies, even the insights of my own city past, I do so only, solely, and entirely that I might look well at the creek. You don't run down the present, pursue it with baited hooks and nets. You wait for it, empty-handed, and you are filled. You'll have fish left over. The creek is the one great giver. It is, by definition, Christmas, the incarnation. This old rock planet gets the present for a present on its birthday every day.

Here is the word from a subatomic physicist: "Everything that has already happened is particles, everything in the future is waves." Let me twist his meaning. Here it comes. The particles are broken; the waves are translucent, laving, roiling with beauty like sharks. The present is the wave that explodes over my head, flinging the air with particles at the height of its breathless unroll; it is the live water and light that bears from undisclosed sources the freshest news, renewed and renewing, world without end.

Guy
Murchie

THE SEVEN MYSTERIES OF LIFE

My thoughts return now to music, which seems to voice so perfectly the essence of the world I see below me. For your blue-swirled Earth down there is not merely a thing. It also lives through time. And in living, it is not so much an object, in three dimensions, as an event, in four. Its nature in fact resembles that of a melody which takes time to play and therefore exists not whole at any moment but rather strings itself out into a patterned sequence over a mortal span.

Any such span naturally has a beginning and an end, for that is the way with mortality, and mortality obviously is as much an attribute of music as of worlds in this pretranscendent phase of life. Indeed were any earthly melody to play unceasingly, whatever beauty it possessed would inexorably degrade into monotony and its once graceful form would bloat like a body with cancer. This rule is broad enough to include at least the vegetables and animals of Earth, who also need their gracious finales — as don't we all?

And in the larger view, beyond this nether finitude, we must ever remember that, as Buddha so succinctly put it, "It is not in the body of the lute that one finds the true abode of music." Almost any intuitive person who has had much experience riding a motorcycle, flying an airplane or handling some other sensitive vehicle knows that there comes a point where the driver begins to forget the mechanism and play it direct, as if the body of the machine were part of his own body and its limbs connected directly to his will. In music the great Arturo Toscanini was a supreme example of this transcendence of instrumentation when he bypassed all technique in exhorting his musicians to "Play not with your instruments but with your hearts!"

A seer like Thoreau would have known exactly what was meant, for he had more than ears to listen with and was always tuning in on, or wondering about, something new and beautiful. "As I climbed the hill again toward my old beanfield," he wrote, "I listened to the ancient, familiar, immortal, dear cricket sound under all others, hearing at first some distinct chirps; but when these ceased I was aware of the general earth-song, which my hearing had not heard . . . and I wondered if behind or beneath this there was not some other chant yet more universal . . ."

What chant, I wonder? Could it have been the forest air, whispering, "Breathe me and live." Or some gentle raindrops surrendering themselves with a sigh to the waters of the pond? Might it have been the Pythagorean octave, a withy consonance of small branches tossing among great trees to symbolize the man-woman, bass-soprano interval of life and harmony? Was it the moan of a blind planet groping for purpose in a boundless universe? Or a divine thought surging through the thresh of time?

All of us beings here are cells of the unknown essence of our world, nodes of flesh that could as well be notes of melody. We are part of something infinite and eternal. There is no boundary between us and the world. In a profoundly relative sense, each of us, as Alan Watts has suggested, may simultaneously occupy "that particular focal point through which the entire universe is singing at this moment."

Are we then God's dream set to music in the place where the sea and the wind have begun to awake and think? Grateful for our blessings, even when they hurt, we trust the world is not paining needlessly for our sweet incertitudes 'twixt desire and reason. We would wish to be wiser and more loving but, for good or ill, our memories are young in this ancient oasis. And we comprehend little. How indeed could a part hear the Whole, or a note the Melody?

Yet the silence of space that enwombs the earth is not totally void. Indeed it is now revealed to be latent, pregnant, mystic — even as it was in the beginning that had no beginning — even as it will be in the end that can have no end. For this is the secret of the spirit that is the life of the form that is the language of the spirit — the eternal spirit that somewhere, somehow, found its voice, took wing and came alive.

Hyemeyohsts Storm

"JUMPING MOUSE"

Once there was a Mouse ... He was a Busy Mouse, Searching Everywhere, Touching his Whiskers to the Grass, and Looking. He was Busy as all Mice are, Busy with Mice things. But Once in a while he would Hear an odd Sound. He would lift his Head, Squinting hard to See, his Whiskers Wiggling in the Air, and he would Wonder. One Day he Scurried up to a fellow Mouse and asked him, "Do you Hear a Roaring in your Ears, my Brother?"

"No, no," answered the Other Mouse, not Lifting his Busy Nose from the Ground. "I Hear Nothing. I am Busy now. Talk to me Later."

He asked Another Mouse the same Question and the Mouse Looked at him Strangely. "Are you Foolish in your Head? What Sound?" he asked and Slipped into a Hole in a Fallen Cottonwood Tree.

The little Mouse shrugged his Whiskers and Busied himself again, Determined to Forget the Whole Matter. But there was that Roaring again. It was faint, very faint, but it was there! One Day, he Decided to investigate the Sound just a little. Leaving the Other Busy Mice, he Scurried a little Way away and Listened again. There It was! He was Listening hard when suddenly, Someone said Hello.

"Hello, little Brother," the Voice said, and Mouse almost Jumped right Out of his Skin. He Arched his Back and Tail and was about to Run.

"Hello," again said the Voice. "It is I, Brother Raccoon." And sure enough, It was! "What are you Doing Here all by yourself, little Brother?" asked the Raccoon. The Mouse blushed, and put his Nose almost to the Ground. "I Hear a Roaring in my Ears and I am Investigating it," he answered timidly.

"A Roaring in your Ears?" replied the Raccoon as he Sat Down with him. "What you Hear, little Brother, is the River."

"The River?" Mouse asked curiously. "What is a River?"

"Walk with me and I will Show you the River," Raccoon said.

Little Mouse was terribly Afraid, but he was Determined to Find Out Once and for All about the Roaring. "I can Return to my Work," he thought, "after this thing is Settled, and possibly this thing may Aid me in All my Busy Examining and Collecting. And my Brothers All said it was Nothing. I will Show them. I will Ask Raccoon to Return with me and I will have Proof."

"All Right Raccoon, my Brother," said Mouse. "Lead on to the River. I will Walk with you." . . .

Little Mouse Walked with Raccoon. His little Heart was Pounding in his Breast. The Raccoon was Taking him upon Strange Paths and little Mouse Smelled the Scent of many things that had Gone by this Way. Many times he became so Frightened he almost Turned Back. Finally, they Came to the River! It was Huge and Breathtaking, Deep and Clear in Places, and Murky in Others. Little Mouse was unable to See Across it because it was so Great. It Roared, Sang, Cried, and Thundered on its Course. Little Mouse Saw Great and Little Pieces of the World Carried Along on its Surface.

"It is Powerful!" little Mouse said, Fumbling for Words.

"It is a Great thing," answered the Raccoon, "but here, let me Introduce you to a Friend."

In a Smoother, Shallower Place was a Lily Pad, Bright and Green. Sitting upon it was a Frog, almost as Green as the Pad it sat on. The Frog's White Belly stood out Clearly.

"Hello, little Brother," said the Frog. "Welcome to the River."

"I must Leave you Now," cut in Raccoon, "but do not Fear, little Brother, for Frog will Care for you Now." And Raccoon Left, Looking along the River Bank for Food that he might Wash and Eat.

Little Mouse Approached the Water and Looked into it. He saw a Frightened Mouse Reflected there.

"Who are You?" little Mouse asked the Reflection. "Are you not Afraid being that Far out into the Great River?"

"No," answered the Frog, "I am not Afraid. I have

been Given the Gift from Birth to Live both Above and Within the River. When Winter Man Comes and Freezes this Medicine, I cannot be Seen. But all the while Thunderbird Flies, I am here. To Visit me, One must Come when the World is Green. I, my Brother, am the Keeper of the Water.

"Amazing!" little Mouse said at last, again Fumbling for Words.

"Would you like to have some Medicine Power?" Frog asked.

"Medicine Power? Me?" asked little Mouse. "Yes, yes! If it is Possible."

"Then Crouch as Low as you Can, and then Jump as High as you are Able! You will have your Medicine!" Frog said.

Little Mouse did as he was Instructed. He Crouched as Low as he Could and Jumped. And when he did, his Eyes Saw the Sacred Mountains . . .

Little Mouse could hardly Believe his Eyes. But there They were! But then he Fell back to Earth, and he Landed in the River! . . .

Little Mouse became Frightened and Scrambled back to the Bank. He was Wet and Frightened nearly to Death.

"You have Tricked me," little Mouse Screamed at the Frog!

"Wait," said the Frog. "You are not Harmed. Do not let your Fear and Anger Blind you. What did you See?"

"I," Mouse stammered, "I, I Saw the Sacred Mountains!"

"And you have a New Name!" Frog said. "It is

Jumping Mouse."

"Thank you. Thank you." Jumping Mouse said, and Thanked him again. "I want to Return to my People and Tell them of this thing that has Happened to me."

"Go. Go then," Frog said. "Return to your People. It is Easy to Find them. Keep the Sound of the Medicine River to the Back of your Head. Go Opposite to the Sound and you will Find your Brother Mice."

Jumping Mouse Returned to the World of the Mice. But he Found Disappointment. No One would Listen to him. And because he was Wet, and had no Way of explaining it because there had been no Rain, many of the other Mice were Afraid of him. They believed he had been Spat from the Mouth of Another Animal that had Tried to Eat him. And they all Knew that if he had not been Food for the One who Wanted him, then he must also be Poison for them.

Jumping mouse Lived again among his People, but he could not Forget his Vision of the Sacred Mountains . . .

Jumping Mouse went to the Edge of the Place of Mice and Looked out onto the Prairie. He Looked up for Eagles. The Sky was Full of many Spots, each One an Eagle. But he was Determined to Go to the Sacred Mountains. He Gathered All of his Courage and Ran just as Fast as he Could onto the Prairie. His little Heart Pounded with Excitement and Fear.

He Ran until he Came to a Stand of Sage. He was Resting and trying to Catch his Breath when he Saw an Old Mouse. The Patch of Sage Old Mouse Lived in was a Haven for Mice. Seeds were Plentiful and there was Nesting Material and many things to be Busy with.

"Hello," said Old Mouse. "Welcome."

Jumping Mouse was Amazed. Such a Place and such a Mouse. "You are Truly a great Mouse," Jumping Mouse said with all the Respect he could Find. "This is Truly a Wonderful Place. And the Eagles cannot See you here, either." Jumping Mouse said.

"Yes," said Old Mouse, "and One can See All the Beings of the Prairie here: the Buffalo, Antelope, Rabbit, and Coyote. One can See them All from here and Know their Names."

"That is Marvelous," Jumping Mouse said. "Can you also See the River and the Great Mountains?"

"Yes and No," Old Mouse Said with Conviction. "I Know there is the Great River. But I am Afraid that the Great Mountains are only a Myth. Forget your Passion to See Them and Stay here with me. There is Everything you Want here, and it is a Good Place to Be."

"How can he Say such a thing?" Thought Jumping Mouse. "The Medicine of the Sacred Mountains is Nothing One can Forget."

"Thank you very much for the Meal you have Shared with me, Old Mouse, and also for sharing

your Great Home " Jumping Mouse said "But, I must Seek the Mountains."

You are a Foolish Mouse to Leave here. There is Danger on the Prairie! Just Look up there!" Old Mouse said with even more Conviction. "See all those Spots! They are Eagles and they will Catch you!"

It was hard for Jumping Mouse to Leave, but he Gathered his Determination and Ran hard Again. The Ground was Rough. But he Arched his Tail and Ran with All his Might. He could Feel the Shadows of the Spots upon his Back as he Ran. All those Spots! Finally he Ran into a Stand of Chokecherries. Jumping Mouse could hardly Believe his Eyes. It was Cool there and very Spacious. There was Water, Cherries and Seeds to Eat, Grasses to Gather for Nests, Holes to be Explored and many, many Other Busy Things to do. And there were a great many things to Gather.

He was Investigating his New Domain when he Heard very Heavy Breathing. He Quickly Investigated the Sound and Discovered its Source. It was a Great Mound of Hair with Black Horns. It was a Great Buffalo. Jumping Mouse could hardly Believe the Greatness of the Being he Saw Lying there before him. He was so large that Jumping Mouse could have Crawled into One of his Great Horns. "Such a Magnificent Being," Thought Jumping Mouse, and he Crept Closer.

"Hello, my Brother," said the Buffalo. "Thank you for Visiting me."

"Hello, Great Being," said Jumping Mouse. "Why are you Lying here?"

"I am Sick and I am Dying " The Buffalo said

"And my Medicine has Told me that only the Eye of a Mouse can Heal me. But little Brother, there is no suchThing as a Mouse."

Jumping Mouse was Shocked. "One of my Eyes!" he Thought. "One of my Tiny Eyes." He Scurried back into the Stand of Chokecherries. But the Breathing came Harder and Slower.

"He will Die,"Thought Jumping Mouse, "If I do not Give him my Eye. He is too Great a Being to Let Die."

He Went Back to where the Buffalo Lay and Spoke. "I am a Mouse," he said with a Shaky Voice. "And you, my Brother, are a Great Being. I cannot Let you Die. I have Two Eyes, so you may have One of them."

The minute he had Said it, Jumping Mouse's Eye Flew Out of his Head and the Buffalo was Made Whole. The Buffalo Jumped to his Feet, Shaking Jumping Mouse's Whole World.

"Thank you, my little Brother," said the Buffalo. "I Know of your Quest for the Sacred Mountains and of your Visit to the River. You have Given me Life so that I may Give-Away to the People. I will be your Brother Forever. Run under my Belly and I will Take you right to the Foot of the Sacred Mountains, and you need not Fear the Spots. The Eagles cannot See you while you Run under Me. All they will See will be the Back of a Buffalo. I am of the Prairie and I will Fall on you if I Try to Go up the Mountains."

Little Mouse Ran under the Buffalo, Secure and Hidden from the Spots, but with only One Eye it was Frightening. The Buffalo's Great Hooves Shook the Whole World each time he took a Step. Finally they

Came to a Place and Buffalo Stopped.

"This is Where I must Leave you, little Brother," said the Buffalo.

"Thank you very much," said Jumping Mouse. "But you Know, it was very Frightening Running under you with only One Eye. I was Constantly in Fear of your Great Earth-Shaking Hooves."

"Your Fear was for Nothing," said Buffalo. For my Way of Walking is the Sun Dance Way, and I Always Know where my Hooves will Fall. I now must Return to the Prairie, my Brother. You can Always Find me there." . . .

Jumping Mouse Immediately Began to Investigate his New Surroundings. There were even more things here than in the Other Places, Busier things, and an Abundance of Seeds and Other things Mice Like. In his Investigation of these things, Suddenly he Ran upon a Gray Wolf who was Sitting there doing absolutely Nothing.

"Hello, Brother Wolf," Jumping Mouse said.

The Wolf's Ears Came Alert and his Eyes Shone. "Wolf! Wolf! Yes, that is what I am, I am a Wolf!" But then his mind Dimmed again and it was not long before he Sat Quietly again, completely without Memory as to who he was. Each time Jumping Mouse Reminded him who he was, he became Excited with the News, but soon would Forget again.

"Such a Great Being," thought Jumping Mouse, but he has no Memory."

Jumping Mouse Went to the Center of this New Place and was Quiet! He Listened for a very long time to the Beating of his Heart. Then Suddenly he Made up his Mind. He Scurried back to where the Wolf Sat and he Spoke.

"Brother Wolf," Jumping Mouse said . . .

"Wolf, Wolf," said the Wolf . . .

"Please, Brother Wolf," said Jumping Mouse, "Please Listen to me. I Know what will Heal you. It is One of my Eyes. And I Want to Give it to you. You are a Greater Being than I. I am only a Mouse. Please Take it."

When Jumping Mouse Stopped Speaking his Eye Flew out of his Head and the Wolf was made Whole.

Tears Fell down the Cheeks of Wolf, but his little Brother could not See them, for Now he was Blind.

"You are a Great Brother," said the Wolf, "for Now I have my Memory. But Now you are Blind. I am the Guide into the Sacred Mountains. I will Take you there. There is a Great Medicine Lake there. The most Beautiful Lake in the World. All the World is Reflected there. The People, the Lodges of the People, and All the Beings of the Prairie and Skies."

"Please Take me there," Jumping Mouse said.

The Wolf Guided him through the Pines to the Medicine Lake. Jumping Mouse Drank the Water from the Lake. The Wolf Described the Beauty to him.

"I must Leave you here," said Wolf, "for I must Return so that I may Guide Others, but I will Remain with you as long as you Like."

"Thank you, my Brother," said Jumping Mouse. "But although I am Frightened to be Alone, I Know you must Go so that you may Show Others the Way to this Place." Jumping Mouse Sat there Trembling in Fear.

It was no use Running, for he was Blind, but he Knew an Eagle would Find him Here. He Felt a Shadow on his Back and Heard the Sound that Eagles Make. He Braced himself for the Shock. And the Eagle Hit! Jumping Mouse went to Sleep.

Then he Woke Up. The surprise of being Alive was Great, but Now he could See! Everything was Blurry, but the Colors were Beautiful.

"I can See! I can See!" said Jumping Mouse over again and again.

A Blurry Shape Came toward Jumping Mouse. Jumping Mouse Squinted hard but the Shape Remained a Blur.

"Hello, Brother," a Voice said, "Do you Want some Medicine?"

"Some Medicine for me?" asked Jumping Mouse. "Yes! Yes!"

"Then Crouch down as Low as you Can," the Voice said, "and Jump as High as you Can."

Jumping Mouse did as he was Instructed. He Crouched as Low as he Could and Jumped! The Wind Caught him and Carried him Higher.

"Do not be Afraid," the Voice called to him. "Hang on to the Wind and Trust!"

Jumping Mouse did. He Closed his Eyes and Hung on to the Wind and it Carried him Higher and Higher. Jumping Mouse Opened his Eyes and they were Clear, and the Higher he Went the Clearer they Became. Jumping Mouse Saw his Old Friend upon a Lily Pad on the Beautiful Medicine Lake. It was the Frog.

"You have a New Name." Called the Frog. "You are Eagle!"

Wendell Berry

THE UNFORESEEN WILDERNESS

And the world cannot be discovered by a journey of miles, no matter how long, but only by a spiritual journey, a journey of one inch, very arduous and humbling and joyful, by which we arrive at the ground at our feet, and learn to be at home.

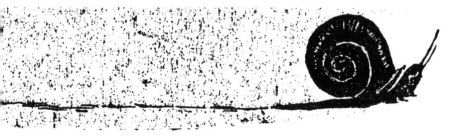

Zen
Verse

If you understand, things
are just as they are;
If you do not understand, things
are just as they are.

If you have enjoyed The Earth Speaks,
we invite you to join and support

THE INSTITUTE FOR EARTH EDUCATION

For over twenty years the public has been led to believe that there is a serious educational response underway in the world regarding the environmental problems of the earth. It is not true. The environmental educational movement has been led astray:

⊕ trivialized by mainstream education
⊕ diluted by those with other agendas
⊕ co-opted by the very agencies and industries that have contributed so much to the problems

In The Institute for Earth Education we have taken a new direction——an alternative that many outdoor leaders around the world have already adopted. It is called the earth education path, and anyone can follow it in developing genuine educational programs of magical learning adventures.

Earth education aims to accomplish what environmental education set out to do, but didn't: to help people improve upon their cognitive and affective relationship with the earth's natural communities and life support systems, and begin crafting lifestyles that will lessen their impact upon those places and processes on behalf of all the planet's passengers.

Unfortunately, many of our environmental leaders and organizations, albeit unknowingly, continue to contribute to the cause of our problems rather than their solutions. Please join us in charting this alternative course, while we still have time to make an educational difference.

Established in 1974, The Institute for Earth Education is a nonprofit volunteer group made up of an international network of individuals and member organizations. We have become the world's largest group of educators devoted to helping people live more lightly on the earth. Our programs, such as, Sunship Earth,™ Earthkeepers,™ and Earth Rangers,™ are the most widely adopted programs in the field of outdoor learning. Tens of thousands of youngsters around the world participate in them each year. Please contact us for a free copy of our annual Earth Education Sourcebook: The Institute for Earth Education, Cedar Cove, Greenville, WV 24945 U.S.A. (two first class stamps or international postal response coupons will be appreciated)

Please note: Our coordinators receive only modest salaries and our authors receive no royalties for their efforts. We have never had any government support, foundation grants, nor industry sponsorships.

CREDITS

THE EARTH SPEAKS/187

S ilently a flower blooms,
  In silence it falls away;
Yet here now, at this moment, at this place,
    The world of the flower, the whole of
    the world is blooming.
This is the talk of the flower, the truth
    of the blossom;
The glory of eternal life is fully shining here.

                    Zenkei Shibayama